W9-DED-160

Pioneers of the American West

Other Books in the History Makers Series:

Pioneers of the American West

By Sherri Peel Taylor

Lucent Books
P.O. Box 289011, San Diego, CA 92198-9011

On Cover:
Center: Daniel Boone leading settlers.
Upper Right: John Charles Frémont.
Lower Right: Stephen Fuller Austin.
Bottom Left: John Augustus Sutter.

Library of Congress Cataloging-in-Publication Data

Taylor, Sherri Peel, 1947–
    Pioneers of the American West / by Sherri Peel Taylor.
      p.   cm. — (History makers)
    Includes bibliographical references and index.
    Summary: Profiles the lives and struggles of American pioneers Daniel
Boone, Stephen Fuller Austin, Jedediah Smith, John Augustus Sutter,
Narcissa Prentiss Whitman, and John Charles Frémont.
    ISBN 1-56006-886-8 (lib : alk. paper)
    1. Pioneers—West (U.S.)—Biography—Juvenile literature. 2. West
(U.S.)—Biography—Juvenile literature. 3. Frontier and pioneer life—West
(U.S.)—Juvenile literature. 4. West (U.S.)—History—To 1848—Juvenile
literature. [1. Pioneers. 2. West (U.S.)—Biography. 3. Frontier and pioneer
life—West (U.S.) 4. West (U.S.)—History—To 1848.] I. Title. II. Series.
    F592.T29 2002
    978'.02'0922—dc21
                                                          2001001158

Printed in the U.S.A.

CONTENTS

The literary form most often referred to as "multiple biography" was perfected in the first century A.D. by Plutarch, a perceptive and talented moralist and historian who hailed from the small town of Chaeronea in central Greece. His most famous work, *Parallel Lives*, consists of a long series of biographies of noteworthy ancient Greek and Roman statesmen and military leaders. Frequently, Plutarch compares a famous Greek to a famous Roman, pointing out similarities in personality and achievements. These expertly constructed and very readable tracts provided later historians and others, including playwrights like Shakespeare, with priceless information about prominent ancient personages and also inspired new generations of writers to tackle the multiple biography genre.

The Lucent History Makers series proudly carries on the venerable tradition handed down from Plutarch. Each volume in the series consists of a set of five to eight biographies of important and influential historical figures who are linked together by a common factor. In *Rulers of Ancient Rome*, for example, all the figures were generals, consuls, or emperors of either the Roman Republic or Empire; while the subjects of *Fighters Against American Slavery*, though they lived in different places and times, all shared the same goal, namely the eradication of human servitude. Mindful that politicians and military leaders are not (and never have been) the only people who shape the course of history, the editors of the series have also included representatives from a wide range of endeavors, including scientists, artists, writers, philosophers, religious leaders, and sports figures.

Each book is intended to give a range of figures—some well known, others less known; some who made a great impact on history, others who made only a small impact. For instance, by making Columbus's initial voyage possible, Spain's Queen Isabella I, featured in *Women Leaders of Nations*, helped to open up the New World to exploration and exploitation by the European powers. Unarguably, therefore, she made a major contribution to a series of events that had momentous consequences for the entire world. By contrast, Catherine II, the eighteenth-century Russian queen, and Golda Meir, the modern Israeli prime minister, did not play roles of global impact; however, their policies and actions significantly influenced the historical development of both their own countries and their regional neighbors. Regardless of their relative importance in the greater historical scheme, all of the figures chronicled in the History Makers series made contributions to posterity; and their public achievements, as well as what is known about their private lives, are presented and evaluated in light of the most recent scholarship.

In addition, each volume in the series is documented and substantiated by a wide array of primary and secondary source quotations. The primary source quotes enliven the text by presenting eyewitness views of the times and culture in which each history maker lived; while the secondary source quotes, taken from the works of respected modern scholars, offer expert elaboration and/or critical commentary. Each quote is footnoted, demonstrating to the reader exactly where biographers find their information. The footnotes also provide the reader with the means of conducting additional research. Finally, to further guide and illuminate readers, each volume in the series features photographs, two bibliographies, and a comprehensive index.

The History Makers series provides both students engaged in research and more casual readers with informative, enlightening, and entertaining overviews of individuals from a variety of circumstances, professions, and backgrounds. No doubt all of them, whether loved or hated, benevolent or cruel, constructive or destructive, will remain endlessly fascinating to each new generation seeking to identify the forces that shaped their world.

Inspired by American "Legends"

The pursuit of adventure and the desire for a plot of land to call one's own remain two of America's most cherished ideals. The people who succeeded in capturing those ideals, primarily during the years of westward expansion in the United States (1780–1890), became legends. Their strength, valor, and resourcefulness in the face of severe trials, resulted in stories that inspired Americans to abandon their homes, pack up their families, and head west. According to historians, "If there is one quality that most Americans share, it is a yearning that sets their eyes straining for a look beyond the horizon, their minds wondering what might be beyond their range of vision, and their feet on the paths into the unknown."[1]

Particularly after the Revolutionary War in the late eighteenth century, Americans wanted to see the unknown, the great expanses that lay to the west. But no easy journey by sea could take them there. No cash payment or paper deed could purchase the land. They would have to take it with fortitude and pay for it with blood. And to lead them there, Americans needed heroes.

The First Heroes

Previously the need for heroes had been met by such men as first president George Washington, composer of the Declaration of Independence Thomas Jefferson, and Revolutionary War general George Rogers Clark. Those days had passed, however. Americans needed new heroes to lead them forward and they found them easily in such men as Daniel Boone, Stephen Fuller Austin, and Jedediah Smith.

Valiant women also charmed the nation. Dolley Madison, wife of the fourth president, saved important documents from the White House just before the British burned it during the War of 1812. And Narcissa Prentiss Whitman willingly left family and home behind. With only her husband and a few companions, she faced an unmapped wilderness in her quest to serve as a missionary for the Indian tribes of Oregon.

Legendary Tales

Before the days of television or even radio, American families gathered in the evenings before bed and on Sundays when the chores had been completed and eagerly listened to stories about these pioneers, men and women who gave up all they possessed, piled their few remaining belongings into wagons, and with little more than a vision and their boldness headed to a new land.

During the 1820s easterners heard that legendary trapper Jedediah Smith had found a pass wide enough to take wagons through the Rocky Mountains and that Stephen Fuller Austin of Missouri had settled a colony in Texas with enough land for all. In March 1836, Narcissa Whitman embarked from St. Louis on a brave and arduous journey to Oregon. In 1846, pioneer John Charles Frémont found himself a guest of one of the greatest con men of the century, John Augustus Sutter, the self-made emperor of Sacramento, California. A year later, as Sutter and Frémont's legends grew larger than life, Narcissa Whitman died in a horrible massacre, at the hands of the people she wanted to help.

Were all the stories true? Perhaps, although today many hardly seem possible. That Daniel Boone actually jumped from the crest of a mountain into the top of a tree or that Hugh Glass, a mountain man mauled by a bear in 1823 and left for dead, survived alone in the wilderness seem incredible. Most historians agree, however, that the truth doesn't matter as much as the telling of such conquests and achievements and the effect they had on others. James K. Fitzpatrick explains, "In a sense, whether the myths are true is irrelevant. They are 'truer' than mere factual accounts, since they represent the high principles and moral convictions of an entire culture—the ultimate realities held by society down through the ages—the eternal truths. The yearning to do great deeds like those of heroes is the important point."[2]

CHAPTER 1

Land, the "Magical Commodity"

The story of the westward movement of the American people is really a story of individual men and women whose lives and exploits shaped a nation. Those lives are a moving and colorful drama of conquest, a surviving symbol of challenges met with courage and faith. Westward expansion was the process through which the United States developed and those who participated in it were part of an endeavor that became the greatest migration the nation would ever experience.

The mass exodus west was a magnificent achievement. For the first pioneers, though, it began simply as a quest for their own plot of land. Their early successes enticed dissatisfied, restless souls from the East and aroused in them the desire for land ownership. These people, tired of their daily routine, were eager for travel, although they knew little of what was in store. Once on the frontier, they faced a primitive life where the emphasis was on survival. Pioneering altered a man's thinking. He learned to adapt, to work harder than he ever had or perish.

New pioneers discovered many things on the road west. For instance, life on the frontier tended to make people equal. Differences in nationality, beliefs, or wealth became unimportant. The impact of moving across the broad prairies, often thirsty, usually hungry, and always afraid molded people's character. Out in the western wilderness, civilization met savagery, and created the people and ideals that evolved into the United States of America.

In Search of Independence

This desire for land and for travel all began when the pilgrims set foot in the New World. From that day in 1607 until 1750, the small settlements of British colonists stretching along America's Atlantic Coast grew into a vigorous, thriving and soon to be independent country. Already the settlers or colonists called themselves Americans. They were poised on the threshold of proclaiming their independence to the world and of affirming their beliefs in the basic rights of all men. That quest for liberty attracted men of all nationalities. In fact, according to historian J. H. Plumb, even British politicians encouraged their sons to "follow the course of the sun to that country [America] where freedom has already fixed her standard and is erecting her throne."[3]

The founders of the new nation had traveled to the New World for other reasons as well. Some were restless and searching for wealth; others were driven by oppression at home, or by a simple search for adventure. Despite those differences though, the first settlers and the young Americans they influenced had one important thing in common. They all wanted a plot of ground to call their own. According to author Bruce Lancaster, "The changing life of the New World land was immutable. Land was the magical commodity upon which prosperity was based, which determined the owner's scale of living and his position in society."[4]

As the first areas settled in America became crowded, noisy cities, overrun by often ruthless governors and legislators, men who preferred to make their own rules pushed west. There they

Driven by a desire for land, pioneers came west by wagon train and found life on the frontier both primitive and dangerous.

could make their own choices and rule their own lives. Thomas H. O'Connor expressed it this way, "Life on the frontier was characterized by great independence and self-reliance; there was no strict code. . . . There on the frontier a man could speak his mind freely and would be accepted on the merit of his own abilities."[5]

The possibility of such freedom enticed people irritated by the confining structures of an encroaching society. Men like Daniel Boone of Kentucky, John Sevier of Virginia, and James Robertson of North Carolina led early movements to settle new lands. Even before the American Revolution, they traveled west, despite the fact that Great Britain had outlawed such settlement beyond the Appalachian Mountains, a range which stretched from Canada to Alabama and formed a western barrier to the eastern states. Many followed, however, and soon the trickle of western expansion turned into a flood.

Forces Behind Westward Expansion

Many important political issues also fed this migration. The Treaty of Paris, for instance, which ended the French and Indian, or Seven Years' War was signed in 1763. As part of the treaty, France gave all her possessions in the New World to the victor, Great Britain. Those lands, which included most of Canada and portions of land near the Great Lakes, became available to Americans. In a few short years, thousands had advanced to Fort Pitt on the Ohio River. By 1780, more than ten thousand families had settled near the community which would become Pittsburgh, Pennsylvania, and five thousand more had followed Boone into Kentucky and Tennessee.

By the time Americans won their independence from Great Britain in 1783, a small portion of the fledgling U.S. population was spread thinly across the vast empty area between the Mississippi River and the Appalachian Mountains. Those settlers were soon joined by disgruntled people who resented the U.S. Constitution and forced taxation by the new government. Also, soldiers who had been given awards of free land instead of pay in the Revolutionary War headed west, followed by farmers, eager to possess the land which was selling for bargain prices. By 1790, more than 2 million people lived west of the Appalachians, and there was still land aplenty for new settlers.

Lewis and Clark Lead the Way

In January 1803, President Thomas Jefferson sent a message to Congress regarding exploration of the Missouri River, an area that

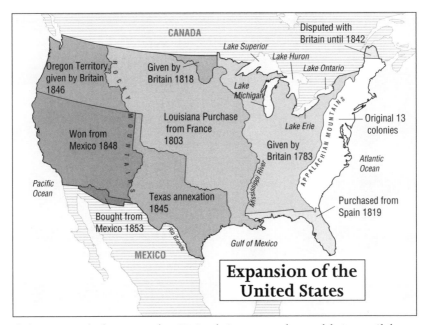

Expansion of the United States

did not yet belong to the United States and wouldn't until later that year. On May 2, 1803, Jefferson made the Louisiana Purchase, buying 820,000 square miles of territory between the Mississippi River to the east and the Rocky Mountains to the west. Jefferson realized early on how important obtaining the land to the west of the then United States was. According to historian David Sievert Lavender, Jefferson reasoned this way: "If France held the land between the Pacific and the Mississippi, and if war between France and Great Britain resumed, England would most surely seize the area. The United States would then be fenced in tightly from Maine to New Orleans. And if so powerful a nation as England closed the Mississippi River, the results would be far more damaging than when Spain had done it. Any such threat had to be challenged."[6]

It was crucial, then, to have reliable information about the western land, rivers, mountains, and people, though Jefferson knew such exploration would take much money and brave men. He wrote, "other civilized nations have encountered great expense to enlarge the boundaries of knowledge by undertaking voyages of discovery. . . . Our nation seems to owe to the same object, as well as to its own interests, to explore . . . the continent."[7]

Thus, Jefferson proposed a daring expedition. He chose two men: Meriwether Lewis, Jefferson's personal secretary, and William Clark, a friend of the president, who began putting together an expedition that would take them across the northern

William Clark (left) and Meriwether Lewis (right) were chosen by Thomas Jefferson to lead a daring expedition from Missouri to the Pacific Ocean.

part of the continent all the way to the Pacific Ocean. When word came that Congress had appropriated the money, Lewis and Clark and about forty seasoned men began their journey. They left from St. Louis, Missouri, which at that time was the farthest western city in the United States. There was no doubt in their minds about their mission. Jefferson had detailed their orders in writing.

> The object of your mission is to explore the Missouri River, & such principal streams of it, as, by it's course & communication with the waters of the Pacific Ocean, may offer the most direct & practicable water communication across this continent for the purposes of commerce.[8]

The troop of men left their camp on May 14, 1804, and marched northwest, searching for the easiest route, hoping to travel by water. It had long been suggested that there was such a river and some claimed to have used it to go as far as Fort Vancouver in what became the Oregon Territory. Since winter travel through the Rocky Mountains was impossible, the men spent the first winter of 1804–1805 in a small triangular grouping of log cabins they built on the Missouri River called Fort Mandan near what is today the city of Bismarck, South Dakota. When spring came, the group again started west and in November 1805, they reached the Columbia River and, two weeks later, the Pacific Ocean. The men returned to St. Louis triumphant on September 23, 1806; their cross-country journey lasted two years.

It was not until 1814 that the report on the expedition, called the *History of the Expedition Under the Command of Lewis and*

Clark, was published, however, since Lewis died and Clark had to hire an outsider to complete their work. Most people learned of Lewis and Clark's hazardous trip by reading or hearing about this book. Fur trappers, though, having already heard of the successful journey west and eager to supply a market greedy for beaver pelts, had begun traveling the shores of the western rivers. Men like Jim Bridger, Kit Carson, Jedediah Smith, William Sublette, and Joe Meeker became famous as men in buckskin, knights of the wilderness, the legendary mountain men. These men told stories of natural beauty beyond belief, of danger, and finally of a broad mountain pass through which even wagons might cross the Rocky Mountains and find the fertile soil of Oregon.

By 1836, the first women, missionaries Narcissa Whitman and Eliza Spalding, had made the treacherous trip with their husbands. Their experiences and the trails they marked further encouraged many who were eager to migrate. Soon thousands made their way along the Oregon Trail, the path which became a regular route to the West and a new way of life.

Oregon or Bust

So many stories circulated about the abundant, productive soil of Oregon that the information was soon common knowledge. Men gathered up their families, packed their worldly goods, bought wagons with rounded canvas covers, and headed west. Oblivious to the perils, their eyes were on Oregon and they were willing to travel more than two thousand dangerous miles to get there.

Most began their journey in Independence, Missouri, where they bought supplies at inflated prices. From there they followed the Platte River to Fort Laramie in Wyoming, about 600 miles west. Another 347 miles later, they traversed the South Pass, a stretch more than 7,000 feet above sea level. By the time they reached the next stop, a fort built by Jim Bridger to aid pioneers on their journey west, they had traveled 1,070 miles. They then drove their wagons 218 miles to their next destination, Fort Hall, where the trail forked. Those who were going to Oregon went northwest to the Columbia River, and those choosing California took a southern route. By the time the wagon train reached Fort Vancouver in the Oregon Territory, the settlers had traveled 2,020 miles, a journey taking around four months.

On the Trail

A day on the Oregon Trail started before daybreak with men harnessing the animals and women starting breakfast. Cooking was

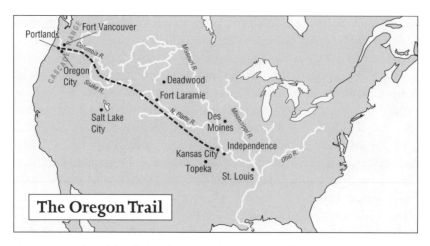

The Oregon Trail

done over dried buffalo dung in the center of a circle made of the wagons. After the morning meal, all the wagons pulled out and began the day's journey. By noon the animals needed rest, and the women built cook fires again and fed their families. Soon the travelers were on the trail again and by nightfall the line of wagons might have traveled as much as fifteen or twenty miles.

Members of those wagon trains faced many trials along the way, although very few were attacks by Indians. Instead, the pioneers' greatest enemy was the region through which they traveled. As the wagons reached the mountains, the terrain grew more treacherous forcing the pioneers to lighten their wagons. Heavy furniture had to be abandoned, creating long miles of wasting, rotting discards. Because of a lack of grass or grain to nourish the stock, oxen grew gaunt and died. Water was hard to find in many places. Children fell under the huge wagon wheels and were crushed, and a sickness called camp fever claimed lives. It is estimated that as many as thirty-four thousand died going west on the Oregon Trail.

Even though pioneers packed their wagons with supplies, they almost always ran out long before the trail did. Narcissa Whitman, for example, wrote her mother on June 3, 1836, that her group had only a small amount of flour left. "What little flour we have left we shall preserve for thickening our broth."[9] Shortly thereafter though, there was no flour at all.

When the pioneers finally arrived at their destinations, they faced the task of clearing land to build farms, homes, and new lives. Even though the land was not quite as rich as the advertisements had stated, most people found Oregon to be a paradise for farmers and homesteaders who did not mind hard work.

Gold Fever

Although the desire for land in Oregon or California had driven farmers and small merchants alike to the West Coast, it was the cry of "Gold!" in 1849 which brought waves of men whose goals were to ravage the land and unearth its treasures, rather than tame and use it. These men came with little more than a pan to sift the sand of rivers, a few essential items of clothing, and their lust for money and fame. Suddenly, California, in particular, attracted and began to fill with hotheaded, ruthless men willing to do anything it took to find the gold they had been told lay on the surface of the ground everywhere.

This gold rush began when James W. Marshall took on the task of building a sawmill on the south fork of the American River near the present day city of Sacramento, California. On January 24, 1848, Henry Bigler, one of the men working with Marshall, wrote in his diary: "This day some kind of mettle [metal] was found . . . that looks like goald, first discovered by James Martial, Boss of the Mill."[10] When John Sutter, the man who had commissioned the building of the sawmill, realized the nugget was gold, he begged Marshall and Bigler to stay quiet, but despite this effort, word spread quickly. In no time, California was deluged by squatters staking claims in every open space.

Pioneers traveling west often ran out of supplies before reaching their destination, leaving them and their animals at the mercy of the land for food, water, and shelter.

The discovery of gold in California brought thousands of men in search of quick and easy wealth.

The report of gold in California brought more people to the West than anything else. In 1849 alone, nearly one hundred thousand people hurried to California. This number included men with shovels and dreams of finding shining metal, as well as gamblers, prostitutes, and unscrupulous merchants eager to profit off the prospectors by selling them necessities at exorbitant prices. Many men, though, found no gold at all, or lost what little they discovered to thieves. A very few became fabulously wealthy and this sharpened the hunger of those who felt the next lucky strike would be theirs. Some died in their pursuit of easy money.

Others, however, discovered a new kind of wealth in California. After the heat of the gold fever left them, many prospectors looked around and sifted the fertile soil through their fingers. They settled down, planted orchards, devised methods of irrigation, and founded profitable farms and ranches. Lured by gold, they stayed for the beauty and the climate. These men sent for their families and made their homes in California.

Final Frontier

By the end of the 1850s the West Coast was well settled. The Willamette Valley, in Oregon, blossomed with farms and orchards; boomtowns like Sacramento and San Francisco became sophisticated cities. According to historians, "the United States had secured its transcontinental realm. First had come the trailblazers. . . . Finally, millions of settlers poured in—from the eastern reaches of the nation and from Europe—to farm and mine the land, to put barbed wire around its grassy stretches, and to build small villages and great cities on its face. The frontier was a thing of the past."[11]

Those who traveled across the nation also reported that the statements made by early explorers that the prairies were uninhabitable were untrue. At last, people began to settle the land between the Missouri River and the Rocky Mountains once called the American desert. The Homestead Act, put into effect in the early 1860s, offered all Americans a parcel of 160 acres of land for a small fee, and in parts of Kansas, Nebraska, North and South Dakota, Montana, and Wyoming, settlers only had to live on the land for five years to make it their own. After the Civil War ended in 1865, people began to fill the plains. New landowners discovered that the area was ideal for raising cattle and bumper crops of grain.

These new settlers also desperately needed a way to market their produce. Thus, wealthy men began to build a railroad. In Promontory, Utah, in the spring of 1869, former California governor Leland Stanford drove in the golden spike that joined the Union Pacific Railroad to the Central Pacific Railroad, creating a transcontinental railroad.

This newly built railroad made the West accessible to all. The wild frontier was a thing of the past. Pioneers had built their homes, claimed their lands, and given their descendants an opportunity that made them a beacon to nations around the world.

CHAPTER 2

Daniel Boone: Legendary American Pioneer

Long before his death, Daniel Boone had become a legend. Tales of his prowess, his fearlessness even in the face of death, and his uncanny ability to find his way through unmarked forests had been compiled, published, and read as far away as Europe. Perhaps some of the stories had been embellished, but the truth of the man still stood tall.

The forests Boone roamed were unknown and untamed. According to one writer, "The country beyond the Cumberland mountains [of Kentucky and eastern Tennessee] still appeared to the people of Virginia almost as obscure as America itself to the people of Europe before the voyage of Columbus. A country there was—none could doubt; but whether land or water, mountain or plain, fertility or barrenness predominated; whether inhabited by man or beasts, or both, or neither, they knew not." [12] Boone also "knew not" what lay over those mountains, but he was determined to find out.

Not only did Boone possess qualities of leadership and bravery, he exhibited a strong sense of fairness and justice, dedicating his last years to paying off the many debts he had made in early life. One historian says, "Boone had a fierce sense of responsibility . . . a yearning for adventure; an understanding of the need for . . . civil standards of behavior as well as a longing for the ultimate unchecked individualism of a woodsman's life." [13] That unchecked individualism made Daniel Boone a man of legendary proportions.

"Dan Will Do the Shooting"

On the banks of Owatin Run near Reading, Pennsylvania, Daniel Boone was born on October 22, 1734, to Squire and Sarah Morgan Boone. Even as a small child, Daniel hated confinement and preferred to roam through the nearby forests. In 1750, after his father was expelled from the local Quaker assembly, the Boone family moved to the Yadkin River valley of North Carolina, where Daniel grew up exploring the forests, his rifle in hand. By the time

Daniel was twelve, other men considered him a superb sharp-shooter and an outstanding hunter. He also quickly became the one to be bested in all contests, wrestling, or shooting. On the other hand, school and long hours in the classroom were unbearable to Daniel.

His prowess proved so great, however, that even his parents admitted Daniel in the forest bringing home meat for the family was more valuable than Daniel in the classroom. When Daniel's uncle protested that he could teach Daniel to spell if allowed, Boone's father said: "It's all right, . . . let the girls do the spelling and Dan will do the shooting, and between you and me, that is what we most need."[14] Yet, in time, Daniel did learn to read and to write, if not to spell, as well as other men of his time.

Daniel Boone blazed a trail through the wilderness to settle the new frontier, and his adventures made him a legend.

Tales of Kentucky

In 1755, Boone served briefly as a teamster in the company of frontiersmen under General Edward Braddock in an expedition against the French, who were trying to take control of the Ohio Valley. There Boone met John Finley, a hunter who had become a trader and who sold his articles along the back trails of western settlements. Finley's tales of the fabulous bluegrass prairies of Kentucky fired Boone's imagination.

Soon after his time in the army, Boone married Rebecca Bryan on August 14, 1756. Boone settled down to raise a family as well as he could—considering his desire to roam the forests. In the spring and summer, Boone spent his time behind a plow, putting in seed, and raising a poorly cultivated crop. As soon as harvesttime ended, though, Boone picked up his rifle, called a long rifle because it had a flintlock with an extremely long barrel which made it accurate at two hundred yards, and headed into the forests alone. According to one writer, "Behind him Boone left a failing farm, his wife Rebecca, a crop of barefoot children and all his cares. Ahead lay adventure, discovery, wealth, perhaps, freedom, certainly, and danger in every rustling leaf."[15]

Kentucky

The Iroquois called Kentucky Kanta-ke, or meadows. The name referred to the beautiful land surrounding an Indian town located near saltlicks which traders referred to as Blue Licks. John Finley had told stories about Blue Licks while he and Boone served together in the army under General Braddock. Around campfires Boone heard that Kentucky blossomed with clover, and that wild game beyond imagination resided there. Some called Kentucky a newfound paradise.

Boone made his first attempt to find Kentucky in the winter of 1767–1768 along with his brother Squire and a friend named William Hill. The three traveled along the Clinch River, which some said led to Kentucky, but they failed to find the land described by Finley. Faced with an unusually harsh winter, the men gave up and returned home without reaching Kentucky.

Six months later, Boone met Finley again. This reunion came at the right time. Game had become scarce in Boone's normal hunting grounds. The population near his home had grown. Farming had become even harder as the soil had lost its fertility. Boone also had many debts. One historian describes it this way, "the American communities of the Yadkin Valley [North Carolina] once again began to grow, and increased settlement drove out the game. Boone found himself caught in a squeeze between his need for income, what with a growing family to support and taxes to pay, and declining skins and furs."[16] The time had come to move on.

On May 1, 1769, Boone again left his home and headed for Kentucky. He was accompanied by John Finley who knew the way through a pass in the Appalachian Mountains called the Cumberland Gap, John Stewart, Boone's brother-in-law, and three other men. After an arduous and dangerous trek along an Indian trail called the Warrior's Path, Boone and his party arrived and established a base camp in the high grass of Kentucky. Of the area, Boone said, "from the top of an eminence, we saw with pleasure the beautiful level of Kentucke [Kentucky]."[17]

Battling the Indians

Despite the beauty of the land, things did not go well for the hunters that winter. In December, a band of Shawnee captured Boone and Stewart, raided the main camp, and took all the pelts

Boone and his companions view the land of Kentucky for the first time.

the hunters had gathered. Boone told the Indians that the group had permission from the Iroquois, a friendly tribe, to hunt there, but the Shawnee chief, whose English name was Captain Will, rejected his argument. The Indian chief wanted to send a message to other white settlers that these lands belonged only to the Indians. Captain Will kept the men's supplies and horses but released Boone and Stewart, sternly ordering them to return home. Rather than obeying the Indian chief, Boone and Stewart followed the Indians and after dark took back the horses that the Indians had stolen.

This only angered the Shawnee who, in turn, followed Boone and Stewart and once again captured them. According to one writer, the Indians, "fastening a horse collar decorated with bells around Boone's neck, forced him to dance for their amusement. This time, Boone and Stewart were tied together with a leather tug and marched north."[18] Boone later managed to break free and escape. However, as a result of this event and the loss of their buckskins, Finley and the others in the group chose to return to civilization, leaving Boone and Stewart alone to recover their losses.

Soon after their release, Boone's younger brother Squire and Alexander Neeley arrived with fresh horses and supplies. The new group numbered only four, a small force considering the hundreds of hostile Indians who also hunted in Kentucky. When Stewart failed to return to camp one day after a day of hunting, Neeley felt he had had all he could stand of days dominated by fear of Indian attack and decided to return home. Only the Boone brothers remained. Stewart's body was discovered five years later in 1775, and Boone concluded that he had been murdered.

Boone soon realized that future expeditions to Kentucky would require more people and supplies to succeed.

Determined, Daniel Boone vowed not to leave Kentucky until he had replaced the lost furs. He and his brother worked tirelessly to hunt and build up a collection of pelts during the winter months. In the spring of 1770, he sent Squire back to civilization to sell what they had trapped and bring back fresh supplies.

Daniel Boone, though, remained alone in Kentucky for three months, unafraid of the vast wild land where he was undoubtedly the only white man for hundreds of miles. Courage fueled this fact and it became part of the legend of Daniel Boone, the man who scorned farming and loved the solitude of the forests enough to risk his life by remaining alone in a foreign land. One writer says that during this period, "Daniel Boone emerged as a full-fledged American hero . . . the explorers' accounts became transfused into mythical descriptions of the continental interior [of America] as an Edenic garden of the world with Daniel Boone its primitive pathfinder . . . central hero."[19]

Squire Boone returned, and the brothers continued their hunting for another winter. When they returned home in March 1771, though, they were empty-handed. Only miles before reaching home, they encountered a small band of six or eight Indians who once again took their skins, their horses, and their remaining supplies. Boone now realized that future expeditions would need greater numbers in order to succeed.

Death Near the Cumberland Gap

Surely Rebecca Boone knew that her husband would soon pick up and move the entire family to Kentucky. She had heard the same stories around the fire on cold winter evenings and certainly understood how Daniel Boone dreamed of Kentucky. Thus, in September 1773, Rebecca packed her few belongings, gathered her children, and followed Boone into Kentucky. Traveling a few days behind them was a group led by Captain William Russell and included several families and about thirty men.

The first hundred miles to the east side of Cumberland Gap took the first group two weeks to cover; they traveled only about seven miles a day. Boone sent his oldest son James, two young boys, and a couple of men to purchase provisions. They met Russell's party and told the captain of the need for more food and of the location of Boone's group. After James and the others had obtained the food and Russell had added his own son Henry, two slaves, a hired man, and Isaac Crabber, an experienced woodsman, to their group, they headed back toward Boone.

Along the way, on October 9, 1773, James Boone, Henry Russell, and the others camped on the edge of Walloon's Creek. Boone's

Boone leads his family and a group of settlers through the Cumberland Gap.

group was camped only three miles ahead of the boys and Russell's several miles behind them. During the night, nineteen Indians attacked, killing the youngest boys immediately. James and Henry suffered terrible torture before being killed by blows to their heads. Only Crabber and one slave escaped the massacre.

Devastated by the loss of his son, Boone left the mountains with his family after the murders. The event was also a blow to the American people. As word of the massacre spread, it inspired a deep hatred in Americans for the Indians and made an already tense relationship worse. The Indians, however, believed they had sent a signal to the whites to stay out of their territory. One writer explains: "The Indians wanted Kentucky for a hunting ground; the Americans wanted Kentucky for homes and farms. There was no reconciling these views. War was inevitable."[20]

To Warn the Settlers

Frightened frontier families took revenge on the Indian tribes around them. According to one historian, "In hope of provoking a war that would silence [the Indians], a handful of settlers began fomenting [inciting] incidents . . . three traders invited several Indians, including a woman with her child, into their trading post fifty miles downstream from Pittsburgh, befuddled them with drink, and cooly slaughtered them all."[21]

The Shawnee, in the meantime, were seeking alliances with the Cherokee, Seneca, and other tribes to drive the white men off their hunting grounds. Lord Dunmore, governor of Virginia, gathered his militia together and asked for two woodsmen to travel across the mountains and warn settlers of imminent Indian attacks. Daniel Boone and Michael Stoner took the job. Stoner was reputed to be one of the best rifle shots in the forest and had been with Boone during the failed 1773 move to Kentucky.

The pair traveled eight hundred miles in sixty-one days to small communities and lone cabins warning residents of the coming war and the Indian retribution that would certainly follow. This mission introduced Boone's name to the public on a large scale, and the people were grateful and impressed. An acquaintance stated that Boone seemed greater than any other man carrying a weapon.

Meanwhile Dunmore organized two expeditions, one under his command and another under General Andrew Lewis. Lewis's men won a bloody battle near Point Pleasant near the mouth of the Kanawha River, and the Indians surrendered on October 19, 1774. Lord Dunmore's War, as the conflict came to be called, ended when Dunmore forced the defeated chiefs to sign the Treaty of Camp Charlotte in which they agreed to allow white occupation of Kentucky. Settlers already living in Kentucky felt secure for the first time, and others planned to join them. These new pioneers, though, would need a better road on which to make the journey.

Wilderness Road

The spring after the war ended, Judge Richard Henderson, a real estate broker, laid out his plans to talk the Indians out of land he desired in Kentucky. Boone would help arrange a conference at Sycamore Shoals to discuss Henderson's plan. Runners were sent to summon the Cherokee leaders to the Watauga River near the border of Virginia and North Carolina. According to one author, "Henderson's company purchased nearly 20 million acres of land from the Cherokees . . . which had been chosen on Boone's advice."[22]

Henderson's treaty, though, was illegal, and he knew it. Tricking the Indians out of their land was not sanctioned by the government. To protect himself, Henderson urged Americans to settle the land quickly, hoping to use that as a basis to claim the land in later litigation, thereby assuring ownership by prior possession. To aid settlement, he hired Daniel Boone to cut a road through the Cumberland

27

Gap to Kentucky for the settlers to travel along more easily. Boone said, "I was solicited by a number of North Carolina gentlemen . . . to mark out a road [the Wilderness Road] in the best passage from the settlement through the wilderness to Kentucke, with such assistance as I thought necessary to employ for such an important undertaking."[23] Henderson also assigned Boone the task of selecting the best site for a settlement and a fort.

To cut the Wilderness Road, Boone enlisted the help of more than thirty men, his daughter Susannah, and her new husband. The job included widening and leveling the path for wagons, moving fallen timbers, cutting trees and vines, and placing logs across the swampy areas to make passage possible. When the group reached the Cumberland Gap, it became obvious that wagons could go no farther. The mountainous region was entirely too rough for wagons. Settlers would be forced to carry their goods on pack animals past that point.

As Boone and his men neared Kentucky, Indians attacked again, and two of Boone's men died. Frightened, a few others packed up and headed home. Boone wrote Henderson giving him the bad news but telling him that he and his remaining men had stood their ground. By early April 1775, the Wilderness Road had been cut. Boone and his men began building a fort on the site Boone personally chose and called Boonesborough.

A few days later, the group faced another possible problem. News reached them of the outbreak of the Revolutionary War; the American colonies were fighting Great Britain to gain independence. The men at Boonesborough worried the British would try to use the Indians to rid the Kentucky area of white men. Frightened, many fled to the east and safety. Boone went back too, but with an entirely different goal. He returned for his family.

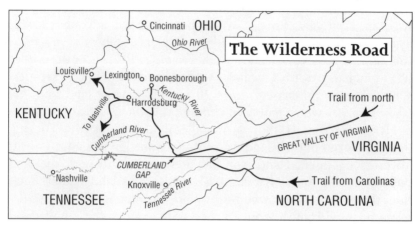

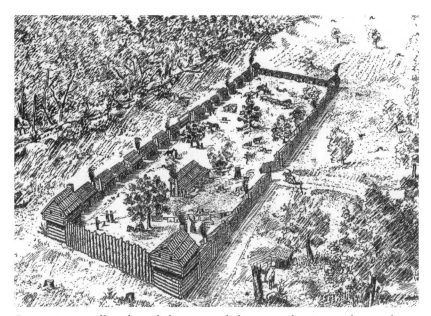

Boone personally selected the site and the name for Boonesborough.

By September 8, 1775, Boone arrived back in Boonesborough with his wife and daughters. According to writer Dale Van Every, "With their coming . . . what had been before a temporary camp of itinerant land seekers had made the vital transition to a permanent community of homemakers."[24] Although others had attempted to set up forts and communities, Boone, his wife, and children became the very first true settlers. They had come to stay. Behind them many others followed, but the dangers, especially of Indian attacks, continued to grow.

Kidnapped

Building a community meant much more than moving to a place, building a cabin, and planting a garden. The community also had to be protected, made safe and secure so the people would remain, grow in number, and prosper. Indian raids, however, made that difficult for the new settlers in Kentucky.

Thus, Boonesborough residents lived as if they were at war. Daily activities depended on sentinels who quickly blew a horn at the first sign of intruders. Settlers remained behind the walls of the fort, nervous, and irritable at not being able to move freely.

One day, Boone's fourteen-year-old daughter Jemima was given permission to paddle her canoe along the river with two girlfriends, but she was warned to stay within a few feet of the fort. The girls did not heed the warning, though, and ended up on the farther shore, where Indians waited. Grabbing Jemima and her friends, the Indians hurried away heading for an Indian village two days distant.

Boone's actions after his daughter's capture further fed the legends about him. With unerring skill he trailed the Indians through thick forests until he knew their destination. After two almost unendurable days of searching, Boone and his men found the Indians' trail and discovered their camp nearby. Writer James Fitzpatrick describes the battle that followed: "Boone's men swept into the camp after the first round of fire. There were a few moments of savage hand-to-hand fighting with the Indians . . . one threw a tomahawk at the girls . . . and others threw knives before scampering for cover. The girls were taken back to Boonesborough and greeted with jubilation."[25]

Time and again the Indians, namely Shawnee chief Blackfish, organized attacks on the settlers. The last blow came in 1778

Jemima Boone and her friends scramble away from their captors as her father and his men open fire.

when Boone led a small party of men out on what should have been a short trip to acquire salt needed to preserve what meats they had available. The Indians attacked, and the people of Boonesborough believed they had lost their gallant leader.

A Captive of Blackfish

On January 8, 1778, Boone left Boonesborough with thirty-two men. While the men boiled saltwater to make salt, Boone hunted the forests for meat. One morning in February, he found himself surrounded by hostile Indians. They took him and his men captive and led them away to their villages.

Meanwhile, the men and women remaining behind at the fort believed Boone and the others had died. Many, including some of Boone's own family, gathered up their things and hurried back east. Jemima remained, however, refusing to desert her father after his rescue of her. Even Rebecca, Boone's wife, left Boonesborough, crossing the mountains to await word of whether Boone survived, or if his body would be found.

For seven months, Boone remained in captivity. He spent his days gaining the confidence of the Indians, even being adopted into the tribe. At all times, though, he was looking for a chance to escape. When he overheard a discussion of an attack on Boonesborough, he gathered food, slipped away from the Indians and traveled for four days through one hundred and sixty miles of deep forests back to Boonesborough. When he arrived, Boone helped those left at the fort strengthen their failing defenses. Then he made a bold, decisive move. Taking eighteen men with him, Boone went back into Indian country to meet Blackfish and the Shawnee head on. His group set up an ambush and defeated Blackfish's braves and then rushed back to defend the fort against the attack they knew was coming.

The Indian attack began on September 9, 1778, and lasted until September 17, but the Shawnee could not penetrate Boonesborough. They attempted to burn the fort—but it rained. They dug a tunnel under the walls, but it collapsed. Finally, the Indians gave up and withdrew from Boonesborough. History had been made. Never again would the fort face such an attack. Settlers poured in from everywhere.

Pioneer in Missouri

Boonesborough and the area around it grew steadily. Lawyers came as well, eager to prove that the original settlers had no right to the land because Henderson had bought it from the Cherokee illegally. Boone soon discovered he had no legal title to the land where he had lived for so long. Also, when people crowded in, the game fled. Discouraged, Boone made a decision to move once again. According to one historian, "Disgusted and as restless as ever, Boone in 1799, aged sixty-five, moved on west of the Mississippi to the central part of Missouri and, in exchange for land that he could more surely call his own, took the step of becoming a Spanish citizen."[26]

Boone wanted to live, he said, where he could not see the smoke

Even in his later years, Boone sought to live on wide-open land away from people.

from his neighbor's chimney. That meant a move even farther west to Missouri, a territory claimed by Spain.

Spain treated Daniel Boone well. He received eighty-five hundred acres along the Missouri River. It was during those last years, while Boone lived north of St. Louis that many of the most important expeditions of the 1800s began. William Clark and Meriwether Lewis passed his place on their way to the Pacific Ocean as did explorers Major Stephen H. Long, who traveled Colorado's Platte River, and Zebulon Pike, who explored the Mississippi. Some even recognized the old man who stood on the banks of the Missouri River and watched as younger, stronger men began the dangerous journeys he once made himself.

On September 26, 1820, at the age of eighty-five, Daniel Boone died. His family buried him in Missouri beside Rebecca as he wished, but legend says he is not there. Donald Culross Peattie wrote: "The real Daniel Boone does not rest there. You will find him in all things brave and free. He is in the running of a doe and the coming of the day. He is the wind in the bluegrass, the path like a shaft of light in the wilderness, the Road, the American way."[27]

CHAPTER 3

Stephen Fuller Austin: Father of Texas

In 1806, the population of the sprawling Spanish territory of Texas had barely four thousand white settlers in the three major towns of San Antonio de Bexar, Goliad, and Nacogdoches. The remainder of the vast countryside was a dry, unattractive area with almost no inhabitants. Spanish authority, centered nearly one thousand miles away in Mexico, had little real immediate control. After two hundred years of attempting to build a colony in the wilds of Texas, Spain realized it would take a very special kind of man to accomplish their goals. They believed they found him in Moses Austin, father of Stephen Fuller Austin. Circumstances, in the end, denied Moses that opportunity but Stephen took up his father's dream. According to author Ray Allen Billington, "The son, to a much greater degree than the father, possessed the qualities necessary to carry the plan [of settling Texas] to a successful conclusion."[28]

Stephen Austin ultimately did bring settlers to the region. And in the process, his dedication to those people and the land on which they lived led to his being called the Father of Texas.

Loyal Son

Stephen Austin was born November 3, 1793, to Moses Austin and Mary Brown Austin in Austinville, Virginia, a town named for Moses. Stephen was the couple's third child, but the first to survive

Stephen Austin's efforts in bringing settlers to Texas earned him the name Father of Texas.

past infancy. Later a daughter Emily and a son Brown were added to the family.

Stephen's father owned a lead mine but most of the area's metal had already been taken out of the ground as a result of years of mining. When he heard of lead deposits in Missouri, Moses gathered his family, headed west, and found a new lead mine and, for a time, wealth. In 1810, he reported assets of $190,000, a fortune in the early nineteenth century.

In 1804, Stephen was sent to Bacon Academy in Connecticut for basic education and then to Transylvania University in Lexington, Kentucky. One biographer states, "[Stephen] had been sent to Connecticut not merely to get an education; he was there, as Moses had phrased it, to prepare for greatness in life. For the eldest son of Moses Austin, nothing less would be acceptable."[29] Before Stephen could complete his education, though, his father called him to help with the family business. Moses Austin believed that the most important things Stephen would ever learn, he would learn from his father.

Moses Austin was loud, autocratic, and domineering, a man of intense pride and a terrible temper, but his efforts in training Stephen resulted in an obedient son. Stephen Austin was willing to work hard on any assignment, and his greatest qualities were fidelity and sincerity. By the age of eighteen, Stephen had acquired vast work experience. His father had given him authority over the mine in Missouri, and he took care of various other dealings his father entrusted to him.

The more responsibilities Stephen Austin assumed at the mines, the more he became aware of the dismal condition of his father's financial affairs. Time had depleted much of those assets, and there was a desperate need for a quick inflow of cash to keep the company operating. To that end, Moses planned to send a large shipment of lead down the Mississippi River to New Orleans where it could be loaded on a ship for New York City and markets farther away. He decided Stephen should command the voyage. According to one historian, "In the year he had worked at the mines, Stephen clearly had won his father's confidence. . . . He was ready for a very adult responsibility."[30]

Leaving Home

Stephen left home in May 1812 at the age of eighteen. The trip downriver was long and dangerous. Thieves, Indians, and disease posed constant threats, and the treacherous waterway made travel very difficult. In fact, sixty miles north of New Orleans, Louisiana, the barge struck a sandbar and sank.

Stephen soon learned that the War of 1812, a conflict between Great Britain and the United States, had begun. If he had arrived in New Orleans as planned and sent the lead to sea in a U.S. ship, his cargo would no doubt have been seized by pirates aiding the British. Gratified that he still retained possession of the lead, Stephen returned to the site of the accident, and raised the sunken cargo. Then hurrying to New Orleans, he made several desperate attempts to find some way to ship his lead or sell it.

Such dedication to accomplishing what he set out to do became a trademark of Stephen Austin. For months after raising the cargo, the young man attempted to complete his father's business venture. He negotiated with men far older and wiser than himself and gave up only when he found the war had cut off all markets for the metal. A biographer says, "Austin . . . was what modern Americans would term a workaholic, driven by his quest for success and fortune . . . he also felt a . . . sense of duty and obligation to his fellow man."[31]

"Nearly Indifferent"

In January 1813, Stephen Austin returned home and joined the local Missouri militia, fighting Great Britain. He later served under Colonel Alexander McNair as a quartermaster sergeant. The months Stephen spent with these poorly equipped soldiers was valuable to him in many ways. From his assignment to keep the troops fed and equipped with fresh mounts on short notice, he learned organization and ingenuity. He also learned the importance of well-laid plans in achieving an objective. More significant, he gained an understanding of the role of discipline and just how difficult controlling volunteer soldiers could be. These lessons would prove valuable later in life.

Stephen Austin returned from service in October 1813, and discovered that his father's lead mine continued to lose money. In fact, shortage of money and manpower after the war had made the family's economic situation much worse and the nation as a whole was not doing much better. One historian said that after the War of 1812, "The first great national panic, or depression, . . . struck the United States. . . . Banks everywhere collapsed, including the Bank of St. Louis. Moses Austin, at the age of fifty-four, was wiped out."[32] Stephen, however, refused to give up.

He tried nearly everything to pay off his family's debts, even cotton farming in Arkansas where he opened a small trade-goods store. But his efforts were fruitless. On March 11, 1820, Moses Austin was jailed because he could not pay his enormous debts. It

Serving in the Missouri militia gave Austin the opportunity to learn the importance of well-laid plans and organization.

was a humiliating defeat for the Austin family and Stephen was devastated. He wrote his sister's husband saying: "I shall remain here [in Arkansas] this summer and after that it is uncertain where I shall go. If my father saves enough to support him . . . I shall be satisfied. As for myself I believe I am nearly indifferent to what becomes of me, or whether I live or die . . . unless I am to be of use to my Family by living and then I should be as anxious to live as anyone."[33]

Stephen's father Moses suffered no similar self-pity. He had an idea.

Gone to Texas

Texas in 1820 remained a largely uninhabited area containing vast plains and fertile valleys watered by numerous streams and rivers. Having spent only a few days in jail, Moses, at age sixty, traveled alone into Texas certain that he could bring the family back to their former wealth and reputation. One writer says, "It was perfectly natural that a dream grew in him that once again he could repeat his former career, by following the Spanish frontier."[34]

This time Moses planned to bring people into Texas to form a town, surrounded by ranches and agricultural areas. He presented this idea to Mexican officers in Bexar, and after much deliberation, the Mexican government granted Moses Austin the right to bring in three hundred families. Their reasoning was clear, as author Charles Ramdell explains. "Within the vacuum [of Texas] an unforeseen menace grew like a stormhead. The Comanche Indians . . . roamed at will. . . . Texas was at the mercy of the Comanche."[35] Moses sent the good news to Stephen in New Orleans.

Immediately Stephen Austin made plans to travel to Texas. On his way, though, Stephen learned of his father's death and he was devastated. He wrote his mother: "This news has affected me very much, he [Moses Austin] was one of the most feeling and affectionate fathers that ever lived. His faults I now say, and always have, were not of the heart."[36] Determined to complete his father's unfinished business in Texas, Austin continued his journey into Texas.

At first he believed the permission would be withdrawn, since it had been given to Moses Austin, not Stephen; Stephen's rights to the grant looked uncertain. Ralph Cushman wrote, "Stephen F. Austin endeavored to get his colony settled in spite of unstable reactions from Mexican rulers. One day he was told to proceed, but the next day he was told to wait."[37]

Permission Granted

In August 1821, Austin finally received the grant from Antonio Martinez, the governor in San Antonio de Bexar. For settlement, Austin quickly chose a tree-covered area near the present-day city of Austin, Texas, and bordered by the Colorado and Brazos Rivers. Austin described the land as the best in the world saying, "[It's] as good in every way as man could wish for, land first rate, plenty of timber, fine water—beautifully rolling."[38]

By the fall of 1821, settlers had begun arriving in Texas. To receive land, these men and their families had to agree to certain requirements. For one, they had to take an oath of loyalty to the Spanish king, which made them citizens of Mexico. Also, they had to agree to become Catholic in faith, although the authorities in Mexico City, the country's capital, largely ignored this proviso.

Austin had other requirements and only wanted certain types of people to settle in his territory. According to one writer, Austin's code stated: "no frontiersman who has no other occupation than that of hunter will be received—no drunkard, no gambler, no profane swearer, no idler."[39] Instead, the new settlement desired farmers, ranchers, blacksmiths, and other skilled workers. This code of no drinking, gambling, or swearing merely echoed Austin's personal convictions and he enforced them as well as he could. He

The Mexican land commissioner (seated) and Austin (standing, right) issue land to settlers who, in turn, were required to pledge loyalty to the Spanish king and to convert to Catholicism.

evicted some for undesirable behavior and had some publicly whipped. For their compliance, each farmer received 177 acres while each rancher got a minimum of 1,400 acres.

Mexico City

In March 1822, just a few months after Americans began moving into Texas, Austin learned that his position of authority would have to be approved by the Congress of Mexico. This forced Austin to travel more than one thousand miles to Mexico City. He rushed off, hopeful of a quick action for Texas. Soon, however, he realized things didn't happen quickly in the Mexican government. One author cites the "customary Mexican procrastination,"[40] as the primary reason Austin's business was delayed.

Another reason was that Mexico existed in turmoil. Formerly a colony of Spain, Mexico had just gained independence and in 1821 declared itself a federal republic, an independent nation ruled by a president rather than a king. During its first thirty-three months, the presidency of Mexico changed thirty-seven times, making continuity of law impossible. When Austin thought he had obtained his authorization in 1823, another change in presidents forced him to begin again.

Austin used those months in Mexico City to learn the Spanish language and the Mexican culture. Austin developed a sense of how citizens of Mexico looked at the world and he recognized the significance of their viewpoint. He said, "They [the Mexicans] are a strange people, and must be studied to be managed. They have high ideals of national dignity, should it be openly attacked, but will sacrifice national dignity, and national interests, too, if it can be done in a 'still' way or so as not to arrest [be noticed by] public opinion. [God punishes the exposure more than the crime] is their motto."[41]

Greatest Colonizer

The first year of the colony, while Austin was in Mexico, proved to be extremely hard for the settlers. A drought ruined the crops. There were attacks by Indians and some settlers left Texas.

Matters improved quickly, however, when Austin returned. He organized a militia and made treaties with local Indian tribes. The settlers began to feel a sense of security again. Austin's presence and his leadership calmed them. Of his work as colonizer, one writer says, "[Stephen Austin] was the greatest colonial proprietor in North American history. But he was something more. He was a politician of exquisite skill, who seemed to understand almost any kind of mind he came in contact with—Mexican, planter, or the

Austin traveled to Mexico City (pictured) in 1822 seeking approval for his position of authority in Texas.

Austin was a slim man of small stature who preferred diplomacy to war.

various frontier types. He found out people's weaknesses and worked on them . . . he was entirely sincere. . . . He began . . . as a businessman, but he became something immensely more important: he was a visionary, capitalist, developer, and Father of his People, all in one."[42]

Still, there were many things Austin did not claim to be. He was not a rough frontiersman nor a soldier by nature. A slim man of small stature and quiet demeanor, Austin preferred diplomacy to war. These qualities helped him in Mexico, where he was accepted by the rulers as a leader and a man of integrity.

The Texas colony grew quickly, and in 1825, Austin requested authorization for additional land grants, suggesting that further settlement would provide a more efficient buffer against Indian attacks. The Mexican officials agreed, and in 1827 granted him a second contract and a third in 1828. One reason for this success continued to be Austin's loyalty to the Mexican government and his proven ability to deal with Mexican officials. One writer states, "Austin was a constructive leader in Mexican society . . . arguably more constructive than many native Mexicans."[43]

During those early years, Austin never considered the possibility of Texas becoming either independent from Mexico or a part of the United States. According to historians, "For the most part, the first wave of Americans into Texas during the 1820's were quiet, lawabiding, God fearing people who showed themselves willing to live in accordance with Mexican law and custom. . . . Even when a . . . rebellion broke out in 1826, Austin helped to raise troops to march with the Mexican forces against the American insurrectionists. He hoped this would be a tangible display of American loyalty to the laws of Mexico."[44] Just a few years later, though, that position would change as a result of meddling Mexican officials.

The Anti-Colonization Law

In April 1830, the Mexican government passed a law called the Anti-colonization Law, which forbade any more immigration into Mexican-held lands, meaning, primarily Texas. This dealt a blow to the settlers' confidence in the Mexican government. Using his diplomatic skills, however, Austin was able to temper the reading of the law slightly so he could continue to colonize, but the Mexican government insisted on stationing soldiers in the colony. That meant that, for the first time, the Texas settlements had to deal with the constant presence of the Mexican army. This presence created friction, and Austin feared the loss of all he had built.

Despite these problems, the Mexican government believed it had good reasons for imposing such restrictions. Mexican officials felt that Americans had taken over Texas, and they worried about losing so much land to foreign settlement. Thus, the government recommended sending Mexicans, even convicts, as colonists. Furthermore, new tariffs would be imposed and the Texans would be forced to trade only with Mexico. Government officials also became significantly anti-American, particularly General Antonio López de Santa Anna who, according to historians, "was determined to bring all parts of Mexico under his unified command. . . . Directing most of his venom against the American settlers in Texas area, Santa Anna swept away privileges granted by the Mexican Constitution [and] . . . formally suspended all civil government in Texas."[45]

The Texans, used to the rights and liberties they had previously enjoyed, reacted violently to this decree. At first, they fought only to regain their rights guaranteed by the country of Mexico and requested statehood within the Mexican Confederation. Rebuffed by Santa Anna, though, the situation changed rapidly and drastically.

Meanwhile, Sam Houston, a former governor of Tennessee, who had moved to Texas, began to challenge Austin's leadership. Houston had some military experience while Austin preferred diplomacy to the battlefield. This difference led the Texans to look to Houston rather than Austin for solutions to their problems. When the settlers formed a committee to ask for concessions from Mexico City, they chose Houston to lead their army, and selected Austin to go to Mexico City to represent their interests.

Prison and a Change of Mind

In Mexico City, Austin made every attempt to carry out his mission, but he forgot what he had learned about the Spanish, and he doomed himself to failure. In Mexico, appearance counted more

Texans began to look to Sam Houston (pictured) rather than Austin for leadership because Houston had military experience.

than reality and even suggestions of impropriety were judged harshly. In an October 2, 1833, letter to the officials at San Antonio de Bexar, Austin suggested that the people there prepare to defy the officials in Mexico City. Although he later admitted he had written the letter in a moment of irritation, it sealed his fate. One writer notes, "When this letter arrived in San Antonio, the political officer considered it treasonous, so marked it, and sent it back to the Acting President of Mexico City."[46] As a result, the Mexican government began to watch Austin carefully.

Believing he had done all he could, Stephen Austin headed home. He stopped in Saltillo, the capital of Coahuila, a state in Mexico and visited the commandant general Pedro Lemus, whom he considered a friend. There, on January 3, 1834, Austin was arrested and charged with treason. The 1883 letter formed the basis of his arrest. He was imprisoned in Mexico City and kept in solitary confinement for three months.

Austin wrote home defending himself for the rashly written letter and encouraging peace in Texas. He wrote, "I hope there will be no excitement about my arrest. . . . All I can be accused of is, that I have labored arduously, faithfully, and perhaps at particular moments, pationately [passionately], and with more impatience and irritation than I ought to have shewn, to have made Texas a state of the Mexican Confederation."[47]

Austin spent the next year and a half confined in Mexican prisons. Of the experience he wrote, "My situation is desolate—almost destitute of friends and money, in a prison amidst foes who are active to destroy me and forgoten at home by those I have faithfully labored to serve. I have been true and faithful to this Gov [government] and nation. . . . I am now meeting my reward. I expect to die in this prison."[48]

Despite his worries, Austin was not entirely forgotten. Friends in Texas sent two attorneys, Peter Grayson and Spenser Jack to lobby for Austin's release. Finally, on July 13, 1835, Austin was allowed to leave Mexico City under an amnesty agreement. He returned to Texas with a new appreciation for the freedom enjoyed in the United States, particularly the right to a speedy trial.

Road to Independence

Such an appreciation changed Austin's political beliefs as well. No longer did he desire to aid the Mexican government or seek statehood in the Mexican Confederation, and his settlers agreed with him. They wanted Texas admitted as a state in the United States. Some Americans desired immediate and forceful action, but Austin thought it necessary to become independent of Mexico first. That way, he reasoned, the United States would be in a better position to annex Texas. Austin hoped this action would prevent war between Mexico and the United States.

This hope proved futile. The Mexican government planned to force Texas to remain part of their country, and Austin was forced to reevaluate his policy. When word reached the colonists that the Mexican government was sending troops to Texas for the express purpose of breaking up the American settlements, Austin visited each settlement personally and told them, "War is our only resource. There is no other remedy. We must defend our rights, our country by force of arms."[49]

Immediately the entire colony set up a governing board called a Permanent Council and formed a militia. Colonists elected Houston as commander of the army and chose Austin as an envoy to go to the United States and lobby for support for their revolution. Austin left knowing that he might lose his position as leader of Texas but understanding that his strength lay in his ability to be an ambassador.

On one stop in Louisville, Kentucky, Austin gave a rousing speech to a crowded church explaining the Texans' position. "What are the objects and intentions of the people of Texas? To this we reply that our object is freedom—civil and religious freedom—emancipation from [the Mexican] government and that people . . . [who] have shown that they were incapable of self government and that all hopes of anything like stability or rational liberty . . . are vain and fallacious [false]."[50]

By the end of March, Austin arrived in Washington, D.C., and then went on to New York and Baltimore to plead Texas's cause. During his travels, Davy Crockett, Colonel William Travis, Jim

Bowie, and two hundred defenders were slain at the Alamo, a Texas mission. In Goliad, Texas, settler Jim Fannin and his men were massacred after surrendering to Santa Anna's forces. The news from home was not all bad, though. Sam Houston and his army surprised the Mexicans at San Jacinto, a river in southeast Texas, and took Mexican leader Santa Anna captive. On April 21, 1836, the Mexican president ordered his troops back across the Rio Grande River into Mexico, and Texas was for all intents and purposes a free and independent country.

Home Again

Stephen Austin arrived home on June 27, 1836. Immediately, he began acting as chief diplomatic strategist for the new government and placed his name in nomination for president of Texas. However, his nonparticipation in the actual fighting had undermined his popularity with the settlers; in their eyes being absent during the war damaged his ability to govern. Austin wrote a friend, "A successful military chieftain is hailed with admiration and applause. . . . But the bloodless pioneer of the wilderness . . . attracts no notice . . . he is regarded by the mass of the world as a humble instrument to pave the way for others."[51]

On the other hand, Sam Houston's victories won him a place in Texans' hearts and he was inaugurated as the first president of Texas in October 1836 and chose Austin as his secretary of state. But prison life had made Austin's health fragile.

Austin's run as Texas secretary of state did not last long; he died two months after his appointment.

44

That, combined with a bitterly cold winter, hard work, stress, and inadequate shelter—his room had no heat—brought on pneumonia.

On December 27, 1836, his condition worsened. Austin roused from sleep for just a moment that night and said to those gathered: "The independence of Texas is recognized. Don't you see it in the papers? Doctor Archer told me so!"[52] Shortly thereafter, Stephen Fuller Austin passed away at forty-three years of age. Announcing to the Texans Austin's passing, Houston said, "The father of Texas is no more. The first pioneer of the wilderness has departed. General Stephen F. Austin, Secretary of State, expired this day."[53]

CHAPTER 4

Jedediah Smith: A Knight Wearing Buckskins

Jedediah Strong Smith overshadowed his contemporaries. Historians credit Smith with being the first to recognize the significance of the South Pass which became the gateway to pioneers traveling to Oregon and California. Yet he did much more. According to one writer, "[Smith] revealed the matchless fertility of the inland valleys of California, traveled from the Mojave Desert to the Columbia [River] and made known . . . the route to the treasures of northern California. He . . . was the original California 'Pathfinder.'"[54]

Wherever he traveled, Smith made precise maps and filled journals with notes which he shared with other travelers. He led his men through treacherous areas and survived under tremendous odds, snowstorms, and blistering deserts, yet his manner so contrasted with the rough mountain man image that his companions called him a Knight in Buckskins. Of Smith, one biographer wrote that, "the mildness of his manner and his sense of unworthiness in the sight of God only brought out in relief his other qualities. Jedediah had intelligence he was able to apply under pressure, toughness of spirit, a capacity for endurance beyond that of most men and above all the courage and grace in the face of adversity that men call gallantry."[55]

Early Life

Jedediah Strong Smith was born on January 6, 1799, in the village of Jericho, New York, to Jedediah Smith Sr. and Sally Strong. He was the fourth of fourteen children of which only ten grew to adulthood. His family soon moved west to Erie County, Pennsylvania, and most historians agree that the Smith family probably lived a life like that of other families around them, hard pressed for food and clothing, but close-knit.

At about the age of twelve, Jedediah met a local doctor, Titus Simons, who would change the young man's life. Dr. Simons took time with young Jedediah giving him a firm foundation in reading, writing, mathematics, Latin, and rudimentary first aid, a skill which would be put to good use in the wilderness. The education built in Smith a burning desire to see the places he read about. In 1814, when Dr. Simons presented the young man with a copy of the *History of the Expedition Under the Command of Lewis and Clark,* the book which detailed Lewis and Clark's epic journey across the country from 1803 to 1806, that wish became a burning hunger. In particular, Smith desired to see the Columbia River which cut through Oregon and emptied into the Pacific Ocean. According to one writer, "[Smith] was obsessed with a desire to see what Lewis and Clark had seen, especially the Columbia River. When he arrived in St. Louis, he was carrying a *History of the Expedition* and a well-worn copy of the Holy Bible. Jed Smith was a religious man, an ascetic, a knight bound on a mystical quest."[56]

With the goal of filling that longing, Smith left home and began his career working on boats trading along the shores of the Great Lakes and the rivers of Illinois. About that same time, Major Andrew Henry, a fur trader and William Henry Ashley, a Missourian wishing to cash in on the fur trade, began a joint venture to promote willing hunters. They placed an ad in the area's newspapers and planned an enterprise which would employ men who would take as pay a part of the year's catch. When he read

A monument marks Jedediah Smith's route through South Dakota; historians credit Smith with being the first to recognize the importance of the South Pass.

Henry's and Ashley's ad in the newspapers, Smith answered without hesitation.

Tall, lean, and with clear blue eyes, Smith impressed Ashley, who was interviewing candidates for the company, as a very serious twenty-three-year-old. Not one of the other 150 men who applied reached Smith's level of quality. Ashley quickly identified Smith's potential and added his name to the list of hunters working for the new company.

Trapping the River

Company owners Andrew Henry and William Ashley divided their forces into two groups, one which would travel up the Missouri trapping beaver and another that would trap along the banks and tributaries of the Yellowstone River. Jedediah Smith joined the second group which left St. Louis on May 8, 1822, aboard the keelboat *Enterprize*. The journey upstream was turbulent as the captain fought the river's current all the way. However, Smith related in his journal that his assignment to hunt along the riverbank kept him off the boat much of the time. Smith was an excellent hunter and his ability with his rifle made him the perfect choice to provide meat for the entire crew.

In late May 1822, the *Enterprize* struck a sandbar and broke apart. Yet, even though Smith's band of hunters suffered the loss of their keelboat and equipment, they journeyed onward to Fort Henry, located where the Yellowstone and Big Horn Rivers meet in present-day Montana.

Reading books such as the History of the Expedition *created a desire in Smith to make similar journeys.*

HISTORY

OF

THE EXPEDITION

UNDER THE COMMAND OF

CAPTAINS LEWIS AND CLARK,

TO

THE SOURCES OF THE MISSOURI,

THENCE

ACROSS THE ROCKY MOUNTAINS

AND DOWN THE

RIVER COLUMBIA TO THE PACIFIC OCEAN.

PERFORMED DURING THE YEARS 1804—5—6.

By order of the

GOVERNMENT OF THE UNITED STATES.

PREPARED FOR THE PRESS

BY PAUL ALLEN, ESQUIRE.

IN TWO VOLUMES.

VOL. I.

PHILADELPHIA:

PUBLISHED BY BRADFORD AND INSKEEP; AND
ABM. H. INSKEEP, NEWYORK.

J. Maxwell, Printer.

1814.

The men arrived just in time to begin their winter of trapping. They quickly discovered, though, that the life of a trapper was difficult. Trappers began their day before dawn checking traps they had set in streams the evening before. (The traps worked by catching beaver or muskrat by the leg and holding them underwater until they drowned.) Each trapper skinned his catch on the trail, cutting off the tail which was considered a delicacy, and then scraping the pelts, drying them, and folding them fur side in for transporting. In addition to the workload, winters in the mountains were harsh. One author describes what the trappers endured, saying, "Winds just short of gale force ripped continually out of the north and west, driving snow in furious ground blizzards, mantling men and animals with white that turned to ice. In lulls, the sky was blue overhead, the sun brilliant, but both dissolved into fiery mist under the assault of the wind."[57]

Death at the Arikara Village

In the spring, the trappers were in need of supplies and horses. Ashley prepared to bring two keelboats of supplies upstream to the men who had been hunting and trapping all winter. As the fur company had done in the past, he planned to buy horses from the usually friendly Arikara Indian tribe. When Ashley and Smith stopped at the Arikara village in 1823, however, conditions had changed. Two Arikara had died and several others had been wounded by traders. This angered the Arikara and the tribe wanted revenge.

The Arikara's chiefs, Grey Eyes and Little Soldier, approached Smith and Ashley peacefully, but the two trappers could feel the tension. The village was silent. There was no normal activity. Warily Smith, Ashley, and their men spent the night on the beach, and at daybreak the Indians staged such a severe attack that in moments fifteen of the men and all the horses had been killed. It was during this battle, though, that Jedediah Smith earned a reputation as a courageous and fierce warrior fighting relentlessly to save his downed companions. Smith stood in the forefront, his only cover a downed horse, firing time and time again at the Indians and leaving only when those trappers who survived had gotten off the beach and safely to the waiting boats. A man who fought beside him later said: "When his party was in danger, Mr. Smith was always among the foremost to meet it and the last to fly [leave]; those who saw him on shore, at the [Arikara] fight, in 1823, can attest to the truth of this assertion."[58]

Smith's coolness under fire and all his bravery could not prevent the battle from being a total defeat, however. Despite the losses, Smith resolved to stay in the area, finish his trapping, and deal with the Indians as necessary. Others were not so inclined. Jim Clyman, who fought beside Smith that morning, wrote years later, "I think few men had Stronger Ideas of their bravery and disregard for fear than I had, but standing on a bear [bare] and open sand barr to be shot at from bihind [behind] a picketed Indian village was more than I had contracted for and somewhat cooled my courage."[59] Many others felt similarly and deserted, returning to their homes.

Yet Ashley had invested a lot of money in the mission and was unwilling to abandon it. When the men revolted and refused to go back upstream, Ashley asked for a volunteer to carry a message to Major Henry who was traveling north up the Missouri River with the other half of the trappers. Jedediah Smith stepped forward. He realized the journey would be dangerous. He would have to travel across wilderness where there were no roads and scores of hostile Indians. Still, he agreed.

In response to the message Smith delivered to Major Henry, a group of soldiers attacked the Arikara village, angering the Indians even more. As a result, traveling the river became nearly impossible. The Indians would strike from the shore and boatmen had little defense. This meant the trappers had to hike through the forests to reach branches of the Yellowstone River where beaver were plentiful. Smith led his men through this territory, an area few white men had ever seen. He did so out of duty to the company, but also out of a thirst for adventure. This freedom to wander

After Smith's confrontation with the Arikara, travel along the river became almost impossible because hostile Indians would attack from shore.

where he chose had been one of Jedediah Smith's reasons for coming west. He meant to make the most of it.

The Black Hills and Montana

From more experienced trappers who had long hunted the Rocky Mountains, a range which formed a continental divide from Montana to Texas, Smith had heard time and again about a wide pass through which wagons heading toward the West Coast might travel. He decided he wanted to find this pass and mark it on the maps he carefully updated as he journeyed.

After the battle at the Arikara village, Smith set out in late September 1823, with eleven men cross-country to find a suitable trapping spot and build an encampment for the next winter's hunt. Because they had only a few horses the men walked and the horses carted the traps and supplies. Jim Clyman and Smith's good friend, William Sublette from Kentucky went along. The crew also included Thomas Fitzpatrick, Thomas Eddie, and three men named Branch, Stone, and Rose.

Because they left late in the season, the men were in a hurry and Smith chose a route never taken before. He planned to cross the Dakotas' Black Hills and miles of dry, rolling, uncharted Montana Territory, hoping that along the way his group might purchase much-needed horses from some friendly Sioux. It was dangerous, but the men knew how to survive, and they felt their ability to collect beaver for the year would be severely limited if they tarried too long on the trail.

Hazards Along the Way

One of the main hazards the trappers faced was a lack of water. On the second day, Clyman went ahead while Smith came last in a long scattered line of thirsty, tired men. When Clyman found water, he shot into the air so the others could hurry forward. Most of the men made it right away, but two simply could not travel any farther. They were too weak from thirst. In an act that would become his trademark, Smith left the pair for a time, gathered up water and one horse, then went back for his men. One writer says, "To conserve body moisture and give them a chance at survival, he [Smith] had buried them [his men] in sand up to their necks . . . hoping to return in time to save their lives."[60]

As the terrain became difficult and food for the horses scarce, Jedediah Smith led his men forward to reach the South Fork of the Cheyenne River and finally the Black Hills of the Dakotas. The farther the men traveled, the more danger they encountered. As the group crossed an open plain, Smith ran head on into an enormous grizzly. The bear ripped Smith's head from one side to the other and took off a portion of one ear. His skull lay bare in places. One of the men killed the bear while another received careful instructions from Smith on how to go about sewing up such an extensive wound. After ten days, Smith was well enough to travel, but he bore the marks of the injury for the remainder of his life. Of this time, one writer says, "Lying torn and bleeding at the feet of his men, Jedediah retained a power of decision and a clarity of mind which illustrated clearly why he was their captain."[61]

Finding the South Pass

In November 1823, the trappers set up winter camp on Wind River near a band of friendly Crow Indians. While there, Smith listened to the Indians tell stories about the country to the west, directly across the Wind River Mountains. It was a place, they said, where the streams held so many beaver a man could catch them without traps. Smith wanted to see that country and he wanted to see the broad pass he had heard about from trappers and Indians alike. One historian says, "Jed Smith was so anxious to test the Indian tales of a pass through the mountains that loomed ahead that he started his followers on again amidst the deep snows of February."[62]

The snows stalled them, however, and it was March 1824, before the trip really began. Still, snows remained deep and indeed the men faced storms on their trek along the Popo Agie Creek near

The Crow enticed Smith with stories of a lush, beaver-filled land west of the Wind River Mountains.

today's Riverton, Wyoming. Finally, about the middle of March, Smith came to the broad plain called South Pass.

This was no winding narrow canyon through the mountains as Smith had expected but a broad treeless valley as much as thirty miles wide that eased over the Continental Divide in what is now Wyoming. Although no mention of his emotions on finally reaching South Pass remain among Smith's notes, he undoubtedly felt relief at obtaining his objective, as well as delight in discovering an opening wide enough to allow passage of wagons, traders, and settlers.

Others had seen it, traveled it, and talked about it, but Jedediah Smith understood what this valley meant as no other man did. Dee Brown writes that Smith, "was probably the first man to recognize its significance to earthbound travelers. It was a door to the Western Sea; the Rockies were not an impassable wall, the barrier to land travel and transport that Lewis and Clark believed. Jedediah Smith knew that wagons could roll through South Pass."[63]

Discovering this wide pass, Smith immediately utilized it. One historian reports, "Smith and his party spent 1824–25 trapping along Idaho's Snake River and into Oregon—the first Americans to go that way since the Astorians [the first trapping company to visit Oregon Territory]."[64] Although South Pass may be remembered as the most important of Jedediah Smith's explorations, many other discoveries soon followed.

An Inland Sea

By 1826, Ashley and Henry decided to sell the fur company. The loss of equipment in the *Enterprize* accident, the fight with the Arikara, and many other such incidents contributed to the decision. According to one writer, "Andrew Henry had just come down the Missouri bearing a fair catch but completely disheartened by the effort and bloodshed involved in getting it."[65] Jedediah Smith, though, had amassed enough money to purchase a one-third interest in the fur company along with his friend William Sublette and David Jackson, a fellow fur trapper. The men divided their duties into three areas. Sublette was assigned to oversee the transporting of supplies and people to and from St. Louis. Jackson would take on the responsibilities of field operations, and Smith agreeably accepted the task of searching out new areas where the beaver were plentiful. In short, he bought the right to do what he had always wanted: explore the western lands.

Around the same time, Smith heard stories of a great inland salt sea in what is now Utah, a huge lake filled with saltwater and a river which flowed out of it and led directly to the Pacific Ocean.

One trapper called this river the Buenaventura, and Smith wanted to know if it or the lake existed.

Although no precise record of exactly when and how Smith explored the Great Salt Lake remains, from notes written on maps by other hunters and scattered legends told, historians have pieced together what most likely occurred. Smith broke winter camp in February 1826 and took his party of trappers across Utah's Promontory Mountains. From these heights he could see a huge body of water and the briny tangle of streams that fed into it. Yet Great Salt Lake is eight times more salty that the real ocean, so little drinkable water flowed nearby. The men needed water. Their supply was running low, and Smith knew the group needed to explore the area quickly and leave; thus Jedediah Smith decided to explore the lake by boat.

Historians believe that Smith and his men traveled over Utah's Promontory Mountains to the Great Salt Lake.

He assigned four men to build a bull boat, a craft made of buffalo hides and light, strong wood. The hides were stretched over the wood frame—which might be willow or poplar—and crafted into a shape resembling half an orange. Tallow, or grease from animal fat would then be used to seal the seams. One writer describes such a boat saying, "[the bull] boat was made of three skins, tough ones, from elderly bulls . . . it was eighteen feet long, five and a half wide, sharp (narrow) at both ends, with a round bottom and a draft of eighteen inches."[66]

Once the boats were complete, the men set out to explore the lake. It took them about twenty-four days to do so, and while searching for a freshwater stream and drinking water, they also looked for an outlet large enough to lead to the ocean. Although they searched nearly a month, they did not uncover the Buenaventura River or a water route to the Pacific.

Reaching the Columbia River

By his early thirties, Jedediah Smith had seen more of the West than any man of his time. He traveled even farther west discovering beaver by the millions in northern California and Oregon. He suffered the cold of the Sierra Nevada and the dry heat of the desert. He had explored the Great Salt Lake, parts of Arizona, and southern California. Yet in all those years, Smith had not been to the Columbia River, the place he most wanted to visit. According to author Dee Brown, Smith "wanted to see the Columbia River and follow it to the Pacific as Lewis and Clark had done. On the maps which Smith always kept with him constantly revising as he came upon streams and mountains no other mapmaker had seen, the Columbia River was plainly marked."[67]

Ever the adventurer, Smith headed north from California in early 1828. By July, he and the several men traveling with him had reached the Umpqua River in Oregon. As always, Smith took the position of scout and headed out early one morning to look for an easier route to the Columbia. Two men went along. When the three returned, they found that all their men except one, and all their horses, had been killed. According to a report written by the Smith, Sublette, and Jackson Company, "On the 14th July, Mr. Smith left the encampment in order to search out a road, the country being very swampy . . . on his arrival . . . he and others which were with him, were fired on by a party of Indians, but fortunately made their escape; the Camp and property was all in possession of the Indians, 15 of the men killed, one only made his escape. The Indians who made the attack

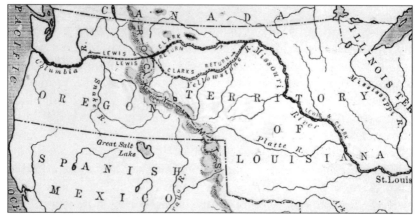

Lewis and Clark's exploration had taken them along the Columbia River to the Pacific Ocean; Smith wanted to follow the same route.

were very numerous; they entered the encampment and massacred the men with their knives, axes."[68] Even Smith's journals and maps had disappeared.

Desolate at the loss of his men, Smith headed for Fort Vancouver, the headquarters of the Hudson Bay Company near the border of Canada. In March 1829, Smith finally made his trip to the Columbia River and over to the Pacific Ocean, but he barely mentions either in his records. Jedediah Smith had changed. During the winter he wrote his brother remarking that he deeply felt the losses of his men. No longer did he hunger to explore the wild west. He said: "I entangle myself altogether too much in the things of time . . . in Augt. 1827, ten Men, who were in company with me, lost their lives."[69] Smith could not forget that those men had depended on him for survival. He had brought them into the wilderness and he felt responsible for their deaths.

It was a sense of responsibility that Smith carried with him the remainder of his life. He no longer viewed the unknown west with the same excitement he had felt in his earlier days. When a young man asked his advice about beginning a career as a trapper, Smith advised him of the dangers harshly. He told him, "If you go into the Rocky Mountains, the chances are much greater in favor of meeting death than in finding restoration of health . . . the probabilities are that you would be ruined for anything in life than such things as would be agreeable to the passions of a semi-savage."[70]

One Last Expedition

Perhaps to help relieve his depression or perhaps to restore Smith's sense of adventure, Bill Sublette talked Smith into going along on a journey to Sante Fe, New Mexico. Seventy-four men left St. Louis on April 10, 1831, in twenty-two wagons drawn by mules. When water became scarce, Jedediah Smith volunteered to go ahead and search for a water hole. Along a dry area between the Cimarron River and the Arkansas River along the Sante Fe Trail, he crossed a small rise and disappeared forever.

Stories circulated that a tall man, who fought bravely before dying, had been attacked by a large force of Indians at a water hole near the Cimarron River. According to the Indians, the man sensed there was no escape, and faced his attackers fearlessly. The man continued to fight even after he was mortally wounded. If these stories are true, and historians believe they are, Smith died as he had lived, exploring unknown territory and leading others through the wilderness.

Although he lived only thirty-two years, Jedediah Smith's exploits dwarfed those of other hunters. One writer says, "Jedediah Smith is an authentic American hero, a man who packed a staggering amount of achievement into the time between his twenty-third and thirty-third years. . . . His countrymen did their best to forget him entirely, but the integrity and magnitude of his accomplishment, the energy and the passion which infused his life and work have finally brought him out on the sunlit plateau for all to see."[71]

Seventy-four men and twenty-two wagons journey from St. Louis to New Mexico. When Smith went ahead alone to search for water, he disappeared forever.

CHAPTER 5

John Augustus Sutter: Gold! In California

Nothing about the hustler style of German-born braggart John Augustus Sutter foretold that he would become an important figure in the history of the United States. More than anything else, Sutter wanted to evade those who knew exactly who and what he was. Yet, although he walked away from debts and barely escaped prison, he settled in the one place in the United States that would become the destination of hundreds of thousands of gold-hungry men—California.

Sutter arrived in California in 1839 to find the Mexican-ruled territory little changed from the days of the first settlers. The coastal lands of California were occupied by cattle ranches, the area's main industry. Hides were shipped from San Francisco to Hawaii and then to other ports worldwide. Sutter wanted to have a large share in that industry, so he built Sutter's Fort near Sacramento, drew in the local Indians as workers, and established a center of commerce. His importance as an official and as a citizen ultimately grew to immense proportions even though his life had not begun that way.

Humble Origins

Although years later John Sutter told a story of royal parentage, his father, Johann Jakob Sutter Jr. of Switzerland, really worked at a paper mill in Kandern, Germany, near the Swiss border. Johann August Sutter was born there on February 15, 1803, and as soon as he came of age, his father apprenticed him to a printing firm in Basel, Switzerland. Unhappy with this work, young Johann ran away to the Swiss village of Aarburg and became a clerk in a draper's shop. There he met Annette Dubeld, whom he married on October 24, 1826. The next day, the couple became parents when Johann August Jr. arrived.

Sutter saw himself as a man of destiny and of greatness, yet nothing about his personality or appearance fit the heroic perception he held about himself. Short and fat, Sutter had never been a man of good looks. Nor was he honest. In fact, he never shunned telling lies if they furthered his goals, and this led others to consider his character shady.

Yet he persisted in seeking social and financial prominence. His first attempt was as a dry goods dealer in Burgdorf, Switzerland. After four years, however, this business failed because Sutter never wanted to reveal his money problems and went deeply into debt. Soon he faced bankruptcy, and in Germany that meant he could be sentenced to prison. Instead, with a forged passport, Sutter escaped across the Atlantic Ocean, leaving his wife and four children behind.

Fugitive from Switzerland

Sutter arrived in New York in the summer of 1834. Immediately, he Americanized his name to John Sutter and worked his way into the upper echelons of society, weaving a new background for himself. Sutter made up a tale about his father being a clergyman

When John Sutter built his fort on the banks of California's Sacramento River, he had no idea the discovery of gold there would make it, and him, famous.

of the Lutheran faith—someone well respected in German communities. He told the people he met in the German-speaking settlements that he was a captain who had attended a military academy where he studied alongside Louis-Napoléon, the future emperor of France, and that he had served King Charles X of France in the elite Swiss Guard. It was quite a story but Sutter managed to pull it off. This carefully crafted identity covered up his long string of debts and also opened up a new world of possibilities for him.

It was during this period spent among the German immigrants that Sutter put into place the pattern he would follow for the remainder of his life: cultivating the identity of an aristocrat. Sutter also began to formulate an idea. Author Oscar Lewis comments, "it was there [among the German settlers] that the thought first took shape in his mind of someday founding a colony over which he himself would have complete control."[72]

Sutter's Dream

Sutter's enormous ego led him to believe this goal would become a reality. While still in Germany, he had read the popular German book written about America by Gottfried Duden. Duden exaggerated the American West, making it seem a veritable paradise. Since moving to the frontier towns, Sutter had been hearing tales of a place called California where the Mexican government, centered nearly one thousand miles away, had little control. Very few citizens wanted to settle so far from civilization and without settlers, the Mexicans had no real hold on the land. In California, Sutter saw an opportunity. It was far enough away from authority to allow him free rein; further, the land had few white settlers and a population of hostile Indians whom Sutter believed he could befriend and use as a source of labor.

In April 1838, Sutter headed west with the American Fur Trading Company. He traveled part of the way with missionaries who were headed to the Willamette Valley. To the missionaries, Sutter seemed odd. He spoke with a heavy foreign accent, sported military whiskers, and had polished manners, wide round eyes, and a big round head. These were not the only reasons Sutter stood out, however. Author Bernard DeVoto says, "He was thirty-five, a Swiss, and ex-draper, an ex-stationer, and a superb liar. Yet liar is an unjust word. He was headed, he was destined for the West, for California—two provinces of fantasy—and among fantasts [visionaries] worthy of provinces he was to become supreme."[73]

Throughout his journey to Oregon, Sutter did everything he could to prepare for his life in California. One author explains, "Wherever he went, he pretended that he had noble antecedents and often managed to gull important people into writing letters of introduction. He had an impressive sheaf of these papers."[74] Those letters of introduction were written statements from the influential individuals Sutter met saying they knew Sutter, and believed him to be a man of prospects. These letters built the foundation of Sutter's future success in California because when he wanted to meet a high official, he sent a letter ahead from someone whom the official knew and respected. Finally Sutter arrived at Fort Vancouver where he'd been advised he could get a ship for California.

With his polished manners and heavy accent, German-born Sutter stood out in the American West.

New Helvetia

By a roundabout shipboard journey, Sutter finally entered California in 1839 at a particularly sensitive time in the area's history. The Mexicans, under Spanish control for many years, had established settlements at San Diego, Monterey, Santa Barbara, and San Francisco. But the number of citizens living in those settlements was very few, and the small communities struggled with a government that was both far away and in turmoil. In 1821, Mexico had declared its independence from Spain and, two years later, formed a republic. Independence, though, did not bring stability; in the first thirty years of independent rule, Mexico changed presidents nearly forty times. According to one writer, "That the overlords in Mexico City had little interest in, and less understanding of, the needs of the . . . Californians was shown in many ways: by the type of men sent to rule over them, . . . by stringent laws . . . and . . . by a refusal to give them a . . . voice in how and by whom they were governed."[75] John Sutter recognized the situation and saw an opportunity to set up his colony. He approached California governor Juan Bautista Alvarado with a proposal.

Already, Sutter had discovered that in order to own property, he would have to become a Mexican citizen, and he began his proposal by stating his intention to do so. Alvarado listened intently to Sutter as he outlined his idea. As a loyal Mexican citizen, Sutter promised to set up a colony in the far interior of California where there were no settlements—most communities existed along the coastline. Alvarado was interested, says author Lewis, because "For one thing, such a colony would be well beyond all existing settlements and, providing it could be maintained, would have the effect of extending [Mexican] authority into areas where it had never before existed. . . . If strongly held and ably administered, it [the colony] could be useful to the government."[76]

Alvarado ultimately agreed, impressed by Sutter's idea and his letters. Promised a grant of forty-nine thousand acres, Sutter left Monterey and traveled north. There he chose property along the Sacramento River and, with men recruited from his travels, put down the foundations of the colony called New Helvetia, after his home faraway in Switzerland.

Sutter had begun his empire. He made friends with area officials and his few neighbors and also ingratiated himself with the store keepers from whom he would need to purchase goods on credit. In an effort to further preserve his image, he also brought out a French uniform purchased on the trip to California. Sutter wore the uniform when approaching prominent citizens, when officials visited him, and when he paraded across his grounds inside the fort. Johann August Sutter, failed dry goods merchant from Germany ceased to exist. In his place stood Captain John Augustus Sutter, builder of an empire. The author of *The American Heritage History of the Great West* says, "From his fort, Sutter ruled a virtually independent principality with its herds and flocks and grainfield, orchards, gristmill, tannery, workshops, and all else necessary to a self-sustained existence. Sutter was generous and hospitable to a fault; his door was always open, and he had a partiality for Americans."[77]

Building a Mexican Empire

After one year in residence, Sutter became a Mexican citizen and was appointed as both commissioner of justice and representative of the government on the frontier of Rio del Sacramento. Sutter had the beginnings of a herd of cattle, which was the main business in California, and had begun training the Indians at his fort to trap beaver in order to supply much-needed cash.

Sutter added more land to his holdings in December 1841 when a group of Russians decided to leave their nearby fort, Fort Ross,

With the purchase of Fort Ross (pictured), Sutter added to his landholdings.

about eighty miles north of San Francisco Bay. Sutter agreed to purchase their 1,700 oxen and cows, 940 horses and mules, and 900 sheep. He also bought several buildings, which he tore down and used for lumber at his own fort, several cannons, a mounted field piece, and dozens of muskets. With these weapons, Sutter could defend himself and his men against all antagonists.

In 1842, Manuel Micheltorena was appointed governor of California, and two years later, Sutter was appointed captain of the California militia and assigned to train troops at his fort. Sutter wrote in his memoirs, "I immediately began preparations . . . I organized and drilled companies, and my fort had all the appearances of a military camp."[78] When a plot against Micheltorena by former governor Alvarado developed in late 1845, Sutter was ordered to march his troops to Monterey and fight for Micheltorena. Pleased with himself, his accomplishments, and his new station in life, Sutter happily obeyed. Although he had told war stories, fabricated a military past, and wore a uniform, this was his first military action.

Mostly the campaign consisted of long marches in rainy weather. Few shots were fired and no men were reported killed. Dissatisfaction among the soldiers grew, and by February, Sutter's troops began to desert. At this time, Sutter came upon a group of his men who were voting on whether they should leave Micheltorena and go over to Alvarado's forces. After a long discussion with them, Sutter realized that Micheltorena had no hope of a victory. Under those circumstances, it seemed to Captain Sutter that he also should switch sides.

When the short fray ended with Micheltorena's surrender, Sutter gained triple the land he already governed. Even though his side lost, by quickly switching allegiance to Alvarado, Sutter continued his prominence in California. Sutter returned to his fort and began planning for his future. He remained satisfied under Mexican rule, yet he knew someday that would change.

Bear Flag Revolt

The United States made no secret of the fact that it hoped to one day possess all the land under Mexican control. By 1844, Californians were convinced that would happen soon. They began to whisper about independence. This put Sutter in a peculiar position. As long as Mexico ruled the area, he continued to serve as a justice under their authority. If he joined the move to independence and it failed, however, he would lose everything. On the other hand, if he did not join the Americans and they succeeded, he would also lose everything. Because he believed the United States was the stronger nation and would soon take possession of all California, Sutter chose to support the Americans.

Far away in Mexico City, previously friendly officials began to question the decision to let Sutter build such a fortification in their country. It made them uncomfortable and they began to plan to seize control of the fort. One author writes, "It became a question of how this strategically located stronghold [Sutter's Fort] could be removed from Sutter's control, transformed into an advance military post, and occupied by a force of Mexican soldiers."[79] The officials had reason to be concerned.

In 1845, John Charles Frémont, a noted explorer, entered California with a force of sixty-two men pretending to map the area. He arrived at Sutter's Fort and placed John Sutter in a precarious position. As an official of the Mexican government, Sutter should not aid the forces of another government. Further, Sutter disliked Frémont because, as one author explains, "by his [Frémont's] actions he had further complicated the already difficult position Sutter occupied in dealing with . . . Mexican officials."[80]

Although Sutter felt obligated to give Frémont the mules and other equipment he needed, he tried to distance himself from Frémont's activity as a matter of self-preservation. Many dissatisfied

Californians and most of the American settlers, on the other hand, began to rally around Frémont.

On June 14, 1845, a group of about fifty Americans from Sacramento raided Sonoma, a town a few miles southwest of Sacramento, and took the leading citizens captive. It was a rash action not supported by most Californians. Nevertheless, they hoisted a flag on which someone had crudely drawn the outline of a grizzly bear and proclaimed independence for California. This situation, known as the Bear Flag Rebellion, meant trouble for Sutter at New Helvetia. Lewis explains, "[Sutter] . . . like others, . . . had been both shocked and disappointed by the irresponsible action of the Bear Flag group, which had outraged the Spanish-Californians and ended all hope of bringing about the change [to independence] by peaceful means."[81]

Following the rebellion, the United States of America declared war on Mexico in 1846. Frémont took over Sutter's Fort, using it as his headquarters; he even made Sutter hold as prisoner General Mariano Vallejo and others, some of the first people Sutter met when he arrived in California. The U.S. Navy arrived and fought alongside Frémont's troops and later General Stephen Kearny's who arrived in time to help end the fighting. Even though a treaty officially ending the war with Mexico was not signed until February 2, 1848, the fighting in California ended on January 13, 1847.

The arrival of John Charles Frémont (pictured) put Sutter in a difficult position; ultimately, he sided with and supported the Americans.

Even before that date, though, Sutter arranged a solemn ceremony at his fort to raise the U.S. flag. In his memoirs Sutter recalled the day: "When the Star Spangled Banner slowly rose on the flag staff, the cannon began and continued [firing] until nearly all the windows were broken."[82]

Golden Discovery

After the war was over, Sutter received assurances from the new legislature that his land grants would be honored, so he got back to business as usual at Sutter's Fort. For the first time, Sutter could see a time when money would not be a problem; his business ventures were stable. Sutter himself recalled those days saying: "After the war, things prospered for me. . . . I found a good market for my products. . . . My manufactures increased and there was no lack of skilled mechanics. I had a number of looms . . . to weave blankets and to make hats. People came to buy leather, shoes, saddles, hats, spurs, bridles and other articles which were turned out by my shops."[83] Travelers could have their horses or mules reshod for a price at Sutter's blacksmith shop; they could buy homemade alcoholic drinks, and eat food grown there—all for the right price.

Sutter also made plans to build a sawmill where lumber for needed improvements could be prepared. James W. Marshall took the job of building the sawmill, a job that would require just the right place to begin construction. In 1847, Marshall traveled about fifty miles northeast of the fort and chose a site, known as Coloma, on the south fork of the American River. Work began in September 1847 and neared completion in January 1848. On the evening of January 23, Marshall let the water flow all night to clear out the gravel and sand. The next morning, he walked the length of the sluice and scooped up a few handfuls of shining yellow metal. According to one historian, "His curiosity aroused, he asked an Indian to . . . fetch him a tin pan. Into it he scooped a few handfuls of sand and gravel from the edge of the stream; then by moving the vessel in a circular motion, he washed away the lighter material . . . there remained in the bottom of the pan a small amount of the yellow metal."[84]

The next day Marshall raced back to the fort to bring Sutter the news. Together they went into a room, locked the door, and examined the small pieces of bright metal. Sutter brought out his *Encyclopedia Americana* and proved that the substance was gold. There was no doubt.

Fear immobilized Sutter. If word got out, men from everywhere would descend on him. According to author John D. Hicks, "Sutter tried to keep the news from spreading, for he feared the effect of a gold rush upon his industries, and believed that the quantity of gold must be small. His efforts were unavailing, however, and by the end of that summer the whole world knew that there was gold . . . in California."[85]

Sutter's plans to build a sawmill near his fort led to James Marshall's discovery of gold.

Despite his fears, Sutter was a perpetual optimist; he hoped to become rich himself mining the gold on the land. However, the placement of the new sawmill—and thus the gold—happened to be off Sutter's land. Immediately Sutter applied to buy that land, quickly attempting a treaty with the Indians but quickly receiving a reply telling him that under U.S. law, the Indians had no right to lease or sell their lands. Sutter had failed. Author Lewis writes, "Not only did Sutter fail in his attempt to have the lease approved; that ill-advised action was also responsible for spreading abroad news of the gold discovery sooner than would have been the case. For . . . the millworker whom Sutter had chosen to take the document to Monterey . . . could not resist the temptation to share his knowledge with those he met along the way."[86] By March 1848, Sutter's entire staff at the fort had deserted and were spending their days looking for gold in the streams around the mill.

Sutter's Fort

Once the most important outpost in the interior of California, Sutter's Fort became little more than a way station to and from the gold fields. John Sutter quickly discovered the impossibility of operating any sort of business in the face of the breakdown of law and order which accompanied the influx of greedy, determined men who took over the gold fields. The men called gold diggers overran the valley, stealing horses and mules, slaughtering cattle for food, and destroying crops that happened to be in the way of their prospecting.

Although Sutter didn't give up easily, he did lose everything in the end. He made several trips to the gold fields himself, looking to make his own rich strike. Failing that, he rented out the empty fort as a warehouse for the more fortunate. When the city of Sacramento began to be laid out in lots, Sutter should have received part of the money from the sale, but one of Sutter's employees stole his portion of the money, leaving him deeply in debt.

Early in 1849, just as it seemed all had been lost, Sutter received an offer to purchase the fort. He accepted the forty thousand dollars and built a two-story house on Feather River in northern California, far removed from the gold fever.

Leaving California

Between 1849 and 1851, historians believe that as many as one hundred thousand people flooded into California looking for gold. Most of them just took the land they wanted without paying for it or getting title to it. As a result, in 1851, California set up a commission to determine ownership of the land. Sutter naturally felt his own title should be safe; after all he had been there since 1839 and had built an empire. He presented his case to the commission and gained approval in 1855. But squatters who resided on those grants began to make their own claims. Later the case went to the U.S. Supreme Court. In the end, Sutter's New Helvetia grant was reconfirmed but his later grants were denied. For Sutter this was a catastrophe, because he had already sold land in that area and would be forced to repay squatters the money received from the sales. Sutter put the amount of his losses at a third of a million dollars.

In 1864 the state of California did attempt to repay a small part of the land money owed Sutter by making him a major general in the California militia and granting him fifteen thousand dollars to be paid over a five-year period. Sutter accepted the money but refused to give up his claims and spent the remainder of his life fighting for what he believed legally belonged to him. After his house on Feather River burned in 1866, he traveled to Washington, D.C., to press his case. During the summers, Sutter lived in Lititz, Pennsylvania. When Congress was in session, Sutter lived in a hotel in Washington and visited Congress every day.

Ever optimistic, by 1880, Sutter became convinced that his petition for up to fifty thousand dollars would be granted. There was a new president, many new congressmen, and other officials would be chosen. Sutter hoped that at last he would be heard. To his disappointment, on July 16, 1880, he heard that Congress would not hear his petition right away. Sutter was devastated by this news. Two days

Historians believe that from 1849 to 1851 (a period of history now referred to as "the gold rush"), 100,000 people flooded into California in search of gold.

John Augustus Sutter spent the remainder of his life fighting for the land he felt was rightfully his.

later, he died, not knowing that Congress had agreed to hear his petition as soon as they met again in the fall.

In his lifetime, John Sutter had owned an empire. His land yielded millions of dollars for others, and although he died destitute, there was no denying that John Augustus Sutter had been a man of vision who went west with a dream and accomplished greatness, albeit at the expense of others. Bernard De-Voto sums up the man and his destiny in California, writing, "Vastness and empire swam in his mind, and for the West of immensity and illusion the hour was quickening. The hour and the place and the man approached one another . . . as Captain John A. Sutter of the Royal Swiss Guards, Johann August Sutter had started West."[87]

CHAPTER 6

Narcissa Prentiss Whitman: Woman over the Mountains

In 1833 an impassioned letter to the editor appeared in the *Christian Advocate and Journal*, a widely read religious magazine, describing the visit of three Nez Percé and one Flathead Indian to St. Louis in 1831 as a pilgrimage to secure religious instruction from Christians for their poor, savage tribes. In part the *Christian Advocate* reported that these American natives had heard "that the white people toward the rising sun had been put in possession of the true mode of worshiping the Great Spirit; they had a book containing directions."[88] The message reached the ears of many good-hearted people willing to dedicate their lives to bring these tribes and others a religious awakening.

Narcissa Prentiss read the article in the *Christian Advocate* and decided that she wanted to evangelize, or teach, these Indians, whom she believed searched for truth and light as found in Christianity. Boldly she wrote the American Board of Commissioners for Foreign Missions stating her desire to go among the tribes and work as a missionary. However, her willing spirit alone could not gain her admittance to the field; no single women would be allowed to go. Undaunted, Narcissa continued her campaign to fulfill her dream of teaching those whom she believed hungered for the word of God.

"To Go to the Heathen"

Narcissa Prentiss was born on March 14, 1808, in Prattsburg, New York, the third of nine children born to Stephen and Clarissa Prentiss. Her father served for a short period as a judge but made his living as a carpenter. Narcissa grew up in a warm and affectionate family surrounded by friends—too many, according to her mother. Mrs. Prentiss once complained that her daughter had altogether too much company, probably owing to her unusually friendly nature. And according to one historian, "the buoyant blonde Narcissa Prentiss . . . [was] pretty, engaging

Bringing Christianity to the Indians was Narcissa Prentiss's dream; in pursuing it, she became the first white woman to travel to Oregon Territory.

and full of delightful good humor—though . . . humor was considered next to ungodliness."[89] She was also very intelligent.

The Prentisses arranged for Narcissa to have an excellent education. She graduated from the first class at the local school, Franklin Academy, which admitted young women in 1827. From there she went on to attend the Female Academy in Troy, New York, where she trained to become a teacher. During those years while she remained at home, Narcissa filled her spare time teaching a class at her church, singing in the choir, and participating in prayer meetings.

In November 1834, she attended a meeting in a Presbyterian church in Angelica, New York, only a few miles from her home. There, she heard the Reverend Samuel Parker speak about foreign missions and felt moved to offer her services to the Indians. Parker wrote to the Board of Commissioners for Foreign Missions asking that Narcissa's request be granted. He said, "A Miss Narcissa Prentiss of Amity is very anxious to go to the heathen [the Indians]. Her education is good—piety conspicuous—her influence good. She will offer herself if is needed."[90] The board, however, refused Narcissa's offer, saying only men and married women would be considered.

During this time, Narcissa met Marcus Whitman, a young man who had trained to be a physician but who also expressed a deep desire to go west as a missionary. When Marcus met Narcissa and discovered her zeal and her good nature as well as her beauty, the two became engaged and decided to devote their lives to aiding the Indians, whom they considered lost souls, since the Indians did not practice what Narcissa and Marcus believed to be the true religion—Christianity.

Narcissa had a long wait ahead, however. Marcus Whitman and Samuel Parker first took a trip west to make plans for the following year's journey to Oregon. Whitman thought it necessary to discover whether or not it would be safe to bring his wife on such a long journey across the mountains. Halfway through the journey, Whitman decided it would. He returned to New York to marry Narcissa and make final preparations. Parker continued on to Oregon, to scout the country, decide where to set up the missions, and report back to Whitman when they met the next year.

Journey to a New Life

In the meantime, the members of the mission board decided it would be safer and more practical to send more than one team of missionaries. Thus, they asked Whitman to choose another couple to accompany him and Narcissa into Oregon Territory. In the winter of 1835, Whitman began his search for such a couple. He knew of one, but foresaw a small problem. The couple was Henry and Eliza Spalding. Years earlier, Henry had fallen in love with Narcissa and asked for her hand in marriage. She turned him down, and he grew bitter at Narcissa, never getting over his anguish even after his marriage to Eliza. When the board first approached Spalding, asking if he might join the Whitmans, he replied, "I will not go on the same mission with Narcissa for I question her judgment."[91] He would soon change his mind.

Marcus Whitman also found Spalding unpleasant, but was faced with a difficult decision when he failed to find another couple. He could call off their expedition or he could go to Oregon with Spalding and his wife Eliza, who finally agreed. Narcissa and Marcus then decided that the importance of their mission superceded their friction with Henry Spalding.

On February 18, 1836, Narcissa Prentiss married Marcus Whitman. The next day, the newlyweds began their journey, traveling overland to Pittsburgh and then on the steamboat *Siam* to Cincinnati, Ohio. Narcissa held no illusions about the adventure before her. She knew it would be a hard journey; Marcus had told her of his earlier travels. No white woman before her had ever embarked on such an overland journey. She knew also that if she succeeded, her trip would become famous and others would follow in her tracks. For that reason, and for sentimentality as well, Narcissa's mother suggested her daughter write a journal in the form of letters to her. It is because Narcissa Whitman kept a journal that people today know about her journey on the Oregon Trail.

A historical marker gives tribute to Narcissa Whitman and Eliza Spalding, the first women to travel the Oregon Trail.

Getting Ready

In Cincinnati, Ohio, the two couples made the purchases required for their long journey. According to one writer: "The grubstake with which each party started was fairly standard. Each adult required: 150 pounds of flour, 5 pounds of baking powder, 40 pounds of bacon (packed in bran to prevent meltdown), 10 pounds of jerky, 30–40 pounds of dried fruit, 40 pounds of sugar, 40 pounds of coffee, along with various amounts of rice, yeast, vinegar, and molasses."[92]

From Cincinnati, the group traveled to Liberty, Missouri. There they assembled their equipment including twelve horses, six mules, and seventeen head of cattle—several of which were milk cows. During the days in Liberty, Narcissa began sewing a large tent out of heavy cloth. Once it was completed, the tent was coated with oil so it would be waterproof and could serve as shelter during the long nights on the trail.

Marcus Whitman had already drawn up a plan of how they would travel to Oregon. The hired men and Spalding would take the wagons and supplies overland to the point where the trail began. Marcus and the women would travel by steamboat, a much easier route. Once the group came together again near Leavenworth, Kansas, Whitman had made plans to join trappers heading to Wyoming.

Since there was less chance of Indian attack if large groups traveled together, Whitman felt the best way to travel cross-country would be for his group to accompany the fur trappers who knew the mountains—and the Indians living there—very well. The trappers' annual gathering took place in the Rocky Mountains—the location changed from year to year—and drew merchants, fur buyers, and every kind of entertainment a trapper might spend his money on before going back into the mountains for another season. Every fur trapper on the continent would be in attendance to sell their furs, purchase needed supplies, and have a good time. From there, the missionaries felt they would have little trouble attaching themselves to any number of trapping parties headed back to Oregon.

Harsh Introduction to Travel

Things began going wrong immediately. The steamboat Narcissa and her husband were set to board in Liberty didn't stop for them because there were already too many people on the boat. Now the Whitmans faced another decision. They could either put off their missionary journey for a year or travel overland alone in hopes of catching up with Spalding. As in all other matters, Whitman made his mind up quickly and stuck to it with an iron will. He gathered up Narcissa and Eliza, hired a team and wagon, and with only a few blankets between them headed out to catch up with Spalding and the other members of their group. This would be Whitman's first crucial mistake. One writer says, "In a frenzy of unfinished preparations they must all hurry overland, under threat of missing [the trappers]. The Oregon Mission came close to failing at the start."[93]

The group had expected hardships, but to be cast out in the wilderness without their tent, which had gone ahead with Spalding, and nothing besides their blankets at night between them and the cold must have been a shock to Narcissa and Eliza. Their trek across country proved difficult and demanding. After two weeks, they finally caught up with Spalding, but still remained eighteen miles behind the trappers. One historian writes,

> The mission party would have to catch up by forced marches or be left behind. To overtake the caravan [of trappers], the need for haste was so great that the missionaries traveled on Sunday [the Sabbath, generally a day of rest], May 22. They crossed the Elkhorn River, on the north side of the Platte [River in Nebraska] on Monday, May 23. The next day they made a hard drive of sixty miles. . . . To their joy they saw the caravan on the other side of the river. They were none too soon for the next day the caravan with the mission party in the rear passed some large Indian villages.[94]

The Whitmans' mission almost failed as they struggled to catch up with the caravan of trappers.

The Trail to the Trappers' Rendezvous

Once the missionaries caught up with the trappers, the march slowed down to a more comfortable pace and Narcissa had time to write of her adventures. Of the company with which they traveled she wrote, "I will tell you what our company consists of. We are ten in number, five missionaries, three Indian boys, and two young men employed to assist us. . . . We have two waggons in our com[pany]. Mr. and Mrs. S[palding] and Husband and myself ride in one, Mr. Gray and the baggage in the other."[95]

Throughout the journey, Narcissa wrote prolifically. She describes herself as contented, happy, and healthier in the fresh air. She wrote her brother advising him to think of her as he rose at 7 A.M., realizing that she had been up before daybreak with the crew. She wrote her family that part of the time she traveled on horseback, sidesaddle. Everything she wrote in the beginning of her journey was positive, filled with her sense of adventure and joy at all she experienced.

On July 6, 1836, Whitman's company arrived at the trappers' rendezvous on the Green River, near Daniel, Wyoming. Not only had Narcissa Whitman and Eliza Spalding become the first white women to cross the Continental Divide on July 4, they also made history as the first white women many Indian tribes had ever seen. Indians and trappers alike treated the women, especially Narcissa Whitman, as a spectacle, gathering around them for a glimpse. Narcissa was, says one writer, "A smaller woman than Eliza, but by no means emaciated, the period's ideal in womanly curves, blue-eyed, tanned but now memorably blonde. Men always remembered her face and her red-gold hair. Men in fact remembered Narcissa, and though she was dedicated to God's service she was charged with a magnetism whose nature no one could mistake."[96] Not only lovely, Narcissa's personality, her friendly nature, and her quick laughter drew people to her.

On July 18 the missionaries prepared to make the last, and roughest, leg of their journey. A small party from the Hudson Bay Company in Oregon Territory had agreed to guide the missionaries. Marcus Whitman, pleased with the choice of accompaniment wrote, "by the arrival of Messrs. McCloud and McCoy [commanders of the trappers' group] we are furnished with a safe and direct escort to Walla Walla [Washington] and have availed ourselves of the company and protection."[97]

Six Weeks to Walla Walla

At this point, a group of Nez Percé Indians joined the missionaries and trappers on the westward journey. Traveling quickly, the

As the first white women in the West, Narcissa Whitman and Eliza Spalding created a spectacle at the trappers' rendezvous, a place where trappers, traders, and Indians traded furs and goods.

group no longer made a noon stop to rest, and Narcissa found it much harder to travel that way. She wrote she "did not know how I shall endure this part of the journey."[98]

Another reason for her discomfort was that Narcissa was pregnant and tired much more easily. Even so, she knew, as the others did, that the worst part of the trail remained to be covered. There would be deserts in the heat of August, the highest mountains to climb, and the most dangerous rivers to ford. Commander McLeod, though, made everything as comfortable as possible for the lady. DeVoto records that "[McLeod] sent her various kinds of food. . . . He got her tent set up before the slower missionary group plodded into camp. He cheered her along the way and yarned [told stories] for her at the evening fire and went out to shoot ducks for her."[99]

By now the group had only jerky to eat, and their meal times were informal. Narcissa wrote to her sister, "Our table is the ground, our tablecloth is an Indian rubber cloth used when it rains as a cloak; our dishes are made of tin—basins for tea cups, iron spoons and plates . . . and several pans for milk and to put our meat in when we wish to put it on the table—each one carries his own knife in his scabboard [sheath] and it is always ready for use. When the table things [are] spread, after having made our forks of sticks . . . we gather around the table."[100]

The travelers rested at night but faced rough terrain during the day. In Washington state's Blue Mountains, Narcissa found herself climbing and descending some of the most terrible mountains she had ever seen. She wrote that as soon as the travelers finished a descent, an even more terrible mountain could be seen ahead of them.

On September 1, 1836, the company reached Fort Walla Walla. Still, Narcissa had to wait until December 10 to move into her own home at a spot called Waiilatpu—the place of rye grass—twenty-five miles away from the fort. When she had settled in, Narcissa recorded in her diary, "I can scarcely believe that we are thus comfortably fixed. . . . We arrived . . . found a house reared and the lean too enclosed, a good chimney & fire place & the floor laid. No windows or doors. . . . My heart truly leaped for joy."[101]

Life Among the Indians

After choosing to dedicate her life to God at an early age, deciding to marry a man she barely knew, and courageously following him twenty-five hundred miles across a wild and barren countryside, Narcissa Whitman and her husband made a tragic error. Their entire course had been decided upon because they had heard the Nez Percé searched for teachers for their tribes. Yet, once the missionaries arrived, the Whitmans chose to live and work among the unstable Cayuse Indians of southern Washington state; the Cayuse

The Whitmans' route (shown here from Leavenworth to Walla Walla) is well documented because of Narcissa's journal writings.

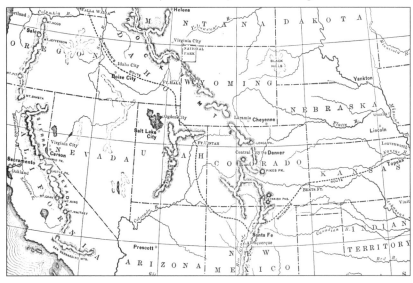

mistrusted white men and resented any intrusion on their lands. Part of the reason for this decision was the continual grumbling of Henry Spalding, who was jealous of Marcus Whitman. It had been deemed essential for the two couples to live far apart, so the Spaldings moved to Idaho.

Still, the trappers and settlers at Fort Vancouver warned the Whitmans that the Cayuse could not be trusted. Narcissa wrote down the comments of the people living in the Oregon Territory saying, "They [the people at Fort Vancouver] do not like us stopping among the Cayouses. [They] say [the Nez Percé] do not have difficulty with the white man as the Cayouses do & that we shall find it so."[102] How difficult, the Whitmans had no idea.

Narcissa began the ministry by holding services in her home and teaching the Indian children songs in English. But she complained that the children were dirty and said she had to continuously clean her house after they left. Despite her requests, the Indians would not build a separate building as a church. As the years passed, Narcissa learned some of the Cayuse language and attempted to teach the Indians to live what she believed was a civilized life. The Indians weren't interested in most of Narcissa's new customs, though, and she, in turn learned to hate theirs. The Indians responded with dislike for everything she represented.

Offending the Tribe

The most blatant and important misunderstanding with the Cayuse occurred after Narcissa's daughter Alice was born in March 1837. At first, the Indians seemed pleased with the first white child born among them and offered a gift. Narcissa refused it. According to one historian, "Narcissa Whitman sometimes seemed . . . lacking in appreciation of customs different from her own. . . . She gave offense on a number of occasions, as when she refused to accept a set of the paws of 'God's Dog,' the coyote, from Chief Tiloukaikt of the Cayuse on the occasion of the birth of her child at the mission. The chief was offended, and in Indian culture when the chief is offended the entire tribe is offended."[103] Although they continued attending the school and church services provided by the Whitmans, the Cayuse refused to accept the teachings because they were offended.

Narcissa's husband also found less and less time to devote to the Indians as he began to cultivate land, build barns and apply himself to the needs of settlers who had begun to move to Oregon. As more and more wagon trains came through Waiilatpu, Marcus

As more white settlers arrived in Oregon Territory, Marcus Whitman devoted more time to their needs, creating resentment and fear among the local Indians.

Whitman spent more and more time caring for the needs of the white settlers. The Indians, in turn, developed a deep jealousy and began to believe that the missionaries, rather than aiding them, actually would displace them.

Tragedy at Waiilatpu

The Cayuse's tolerance of the missionaries came to an end in November 1847 when a wagon train came through Waiilatpu carrying a particularly virulent form of measles. The Indian children got sick and many died. Many of the white children also became ill, but more survived than did the Indians who had no natural immunity to such diseases. Angry, the Indians blamed Marcus Whitman, the white doctor, for their losses. In Cayuse culture, when a medicine man failed, his penalty was death. The tribe felt the Whitmans should pay for the death of so many children.

On November 29, 1847, the Indians attacked. Chief Tiloukaikt came to the Whitman home and asked for medicine for his tribe. When Whitman handed him the medicine, another Indian struck Whitman from behind with a tomahawk. Narcissa took a bullet in her side but escaped upstairs where she locked the doors. Later

The Whitmans and twelve others were killed by the Cayuse who blamed them for the deaths of many of the tribe's children.

the Indians talked her into coming down and when she did, they beat her mercilessly and threw her body into a muddy ditch where she died later that evening. Twelve other people died that day and the missions in Oregon ended forever.

Narcissa Prentiss Whitman died at the age of thirty-nine years old. She had been in Oregon Territory for eleven years working to convert the Indians to Christianity, and despite the tragic end, her efforts were not entirely futile. One author reports,

> by June of 1844 one Cayuse and twenty-one Nez Perces had . . . satisfied Spalding and Whitman that they were Christians. That was its [the mission's] total Indian membership and it moved to the Willamette Valley after that day when an unconverted Cayuse threw Narcissa's thrice-wounded body into the mire and another raised it by the red-gold hair and lashed her face with a pretty beaded whip.[104]

Even so, Narcissa Whitman contributed far more than simply adding a few names to the rolls of a church at Waiilatpu. Her journal, written as she traveled across what would become the United

States, brought strength to many embarking on similar journeys. Biographer Erwin N. Thompson writes, "The name of Narcissa Prentiss Whitman is still remembered. Here was a woman, beset by the faults that all mortals must endure, yet possessing something far richer and greater than most humans could ever hope for. That something was courage—a rare courage that some men experience on the battlefield but one which is not often demanded of a woman. This lady of grace and beauty was dead; but her spirit lived on to inspire the generations to follow. She was of the breed that made the western pioneer a symbol of the strength of America."[105]

CHAPTER 7

John Charles Frémont: Columbus of the West

John Charles Frémont has been called a pathfinder and the Columbus of the West because he went unafraid into the continent's wildest country and brought back efficient, accurate maps that led hundreds of thousands of people to the Pacific Coast during the last half of the nineteenth century. One historian said of him, "Frémont had fired the excitement of a nation with his exploits. . . . Unfurling a special flag after a breathless climb of Frémont Peak in the Wyoming Rockies; risking the Great Salt Lake in a rubber raft; battling snowdrifts; wandering about Sutter's exotic barony; skirmishing with the Indians. . . . The accounts [of his travels] had been practical as well, for they gave the westbound emigrants dependable information."[106]

A contradictory man, Frémont claimed great love for his wife and family, yet spent the majority of his life far away from them, seeking solace and solitude in America's mountains. Although owning one of the richest gold strikes in California and being known nationwide, Frémont died attempting to force Washington, D.C. politicians to pay him for the work he did on the nation's behalf. In spite of his incredible accomplishments, his life began as it ended, stained by disgrace.

John Charles Frémont explored and mapped much of the frontier, allowing many to follow him and settle the land.

"Strange Parentage"

John Charles Frémont was born on January 21, 1813, in Savannah, Georgia. The facts of his birth—his parents never married—affected Frémont his entire life. John Charles Frémont's biographer, Andrew Rolle, says that "Frémont's illegitimate birth and strange parentage—which so long remained in deep shadow—influenced . . . [the] development of his personality."[107]

Anne Beverly Whiting, Frémont's mother, was the daughter of a leading member of the House of Burgesses of Virginia, a very high position at that time. At the age of seventeen, Anne was forced to marry a man twice her age. Still married, she left him twelve years later for a man with whom she lived for the remainder of his short life. The man, Frémont's father, was also named John Charles Frémont and had run away from fraud charges in French Canada. The elder Frémont supported himself as a teacher until his relationship with Anne caused them to move from town to town, often living with Indian tribes to escape public opinion regarding their romance. Frémont ultimately supported his young family by becoming a painter and an upholsterer.

Young John Charles was only five years old when his father died leaving Anne with three children to raise alone on a very limited income. However, family friends helped the young family in many ways. For example, some very important people took an interest in John Charles, particularly regarding his education. The boy had an intelligent and inquiring mind and this, along with a friendly manner, won him many friends. A teacher said of him, "he was no common youth, as intelligence beamed in his dark eyes, and shone brightly. . . . I at once put him in the highest class. . . . Whatever he read, he retained."[108]

One person, prominent Charleston, South Carolina lawyer John W. Mitchell, arranged for Frémont to be sent to a school which would prepare him for college. John Charles proved to be an excellent student, but his love of roving the nearby forests, rather than attending classes, got him expelled from school before graduation. One historian says that Frémont was "a vagabond who sought triumph through adventure . . . and . . . soon disciplinary problems grew out of his love of the outdoors and the excitement of truancy."[109]

This love of wandering and exploring had developed during Frémont's early life when the family lived in a wagon and moved from place to place. His parents had been essentially outcasts, traveling often from town to town and stopping where the elder Frémont could get work. Living outdoors was part of John Charles's life and he was always most comfortable on the trail in later life.

In 1833, Frémont went to work on board a sloop-of-war, the *Natchez,* as a teacher of mathematics. He soon grew bored with that, though, and with the help of some influential friends, he attained a job as an army engineer. In the winter of 1836–1837, Frémont joined Captain W. S. Williams who had been asked by the federal government to map the Cherokee Indian lands. These Native Americans lived where the borders of North Carolina, Tennessee, and Georgia came together. If the West were to be settled, the area must be mapped. As the author of *Visions of the American West* said, "Exploration and enterprise in what was to be the American West, then, began with mapping the headwaters of the great rivers, discovering where they went and how far they were navigable."[110] After the experience of exploring and mapping the wild mountainous region, Frémont later said that he had discovered the path which he believed he had been destined to walk.

Commissioned by the Army

When the survey of the Indian lands was completed, Frémont received some good news, a letter notifying him that he had been commissioned as a second lieutenant in the U.S. Topographical Corps, a group of men assigned to explore and make maps of the American West. Frémont's first job as an assistant to Jean Nicholas Nicollet, a distinguished astronomer and mathematician, would be the exploration and mapping of the vast area between the Mississippi and the Missouri Rivers. Although many men had traveled these areas, none had yet crafted any reliable maps.

Frémont assisted distinguished astronomer and mathematician Jean Nicholas Nicollet (pictured) in exploring and mapping the area between the Missouri and Mississippi Rivers.

Throughout their long trip, Frémont and Nicollet made detailed notes. Later, they would use those notes and their knowledge of astronomy and math to prepare the maps. It was a long and detailed process and intensely important since the people who used the maps would have no other means of knowing what lay ahead as they crossed the country. If the maps led them to the wrong place, it could mean their lives.

After two years of exploration, Nicollet and Frémont returned to Washington, D.C., in early 1840 to complete the actual drawing of the map. Frémont's biographer said, "No document had ever before been based upon ninety thousand readings of latitude and longitude. . . . This achievement earned . . . Frémont the praise of President [Martin] Van Buren."[111] Many prominent men also dropped by to check on how the project was progressing—including Senator Thomas Hart Benton. This man, his family, and his support became an important part of Frémont's life.

Jessie Benton Frémont

It was during the time Frémont and Nicollet were working together that Frémont met Jessie Benton, the daughter of Senator Benton. Thomas Benton believed the only way the United States could claim the area west of the Mississippi River would be to people it with Americans. Because they shared this similar interest, Senator Benton often invited Frémont and Nicollet to dinner at his home, where Jessie and John Charles eventually met.

Satisfied with his chosen work, Frémont had grown into a self-possessed and very handsome young man. One writer said of him, "John Charles Frémont, a young Army officer [was a] . . . flamboyant, adventurer, dedicated explorer and ambitious office seeker."[112] But at twenty-eight he remained a bachelor.

Jessie Benton and Frémont quickly became interested in each other romantically, but Jessie's parents were not happy with the young couple's plans to marry, because of Frémont's background. Because his parents had not been married, Frémont was not considered a proper husband for someone as high-class as Jessie Benton. The Bentons tolerated the young man at their gatherings because he was handsome and intelligent, but they did not want him to marry into their family.

In an attempt to keep the couple apart, Senator Benton arranged to have Frémont assigned far away in the Iowa Territory where he was expected to prepare a map of the river. Nicollet protested losing his best assistant, but there was nothing he could do. Benton's influence was too strong; Frémont would have to go. However, rather than take a long journey, slowly poring over the area, Frémont hurriedly surveyed the river and rushed back to Washington to

Because her parents disapproved, Jessie Benton and Frémont married in secret.

be with Jessie. Then, on October 19, 1841, Jessie Benton and John Charles Frémont were married secretly. When the Bentons were told, they had no choice but to accept the young man even though they considered him disreputable.

Another Trip West

Congress soon decided that another expedition was needed to survey the Oregon Trail, the path settlers took to Oregon. Nicollet and Frémont were once again assigned the job. But when Nicollet became ill, Frémont was left to finish the survey alone. On May 2, 1842, Frémont mobilized a limited expedition. His orders sent him only as far west as the South Pass, the portion of the Oregon Trail through which wagons could travel the Rocky Mountains.

When the expedition reached Wyoming, the explorers learned bad news. Several Indian tribes had declared war against all white men, and American officials explained that Frémont should retreat and wait for another, more auspicious time to make the trip. Frémont, though, decided to proceed anyway. He felt his work, which would guide future families along the trail, was exceedingly important. Hundreds of lives could be lost along unmarked paths. He didn't want to risk those deaths. This decision earned Frémont an impressive reputation, one that would stay with him for life. Even men who chose to stay behind respected Frémont's decision. Frémont's boldness became legendary in the mountains. A man who knew him said, "There ain't a bullet can touch him. That man's got what they call a 'charmed life' . . . of all the public men of that time who led adventuresome and romantic lives, Frémont was the most daring and the most original."[113]

On August 8, 1842, Frémont's expedition reached the South Pass. The group made all the computations and notes needed to map the area and then traveled to the Rocky Mountains to climb, what Frémont believed, was the range's highest peak. He said, "We had climbed the loftiest peak of the Rocky Mountains and looked down upon the snow a thousand feet below, and standing where never human foot had stood before, felt the exhilaration of first explorers."[114] The mountain was later named Frémont Peak.

Finally satisfied with his expedition, Frémont hurried home. He arrived in Washington, D.C., on October 29 and, within a few months, was preparing to go back to the West.

New Route to South Pass

Several politicians in Congress wanted Frémont to see if there was a trail other than the South Pass that could be taken to Oregon. Even though the South Pass was easy enough to travel, the mountainous road beyond it was extremely hazardous. Furthermore, most of the Oregon Trail had never been competently marked. Wagon trains needed trained guides to get them through the mountains.

Frémont's primary job would be to completely stake out the road already being used from Fort Laramie, Wyoming, to Oregon. He had also been ordered to search for places to build new forts along the way. Those would aid in the westward expansion and serve as posts to help settlers along the way. Frémont happily agreed and left St. Louis in 1843 with a group of hardy men. They traveled first to Kansas Landing, now called Kansas City, Missouri, where they would begin the journey across the continent.

Frémont reached the Oregon Territory in 1843. Along the way, he explored many areas including the country around the Great Salt Lake in what is today Utah. In rubber boats Frémont and his men floated along the edge of the lake, and Frémont was the first

Frémont stands on the highest peak of the Rocky Mountains, later named Frémont Peak.

89

explorer to realize that the lake was landlocked and that it did not drain into the Pacific Ocean as had been previously believed. He called the area the Great Basin saying it was an "inland sea stretching in still and solitary grandeur far beyond the limit of our vision."[115]

Frémont and his men then turned northwest and traveled to Fort Vancouver, the northernmost post of the British Fur Company in the Oregon Territory. There, he rested, outfitted his men for the return journey, and then traveled south toward what is today Reno, Nevada. To the group's right, the Sierra Nevada appeared. Beyond it was California.

Historians disagree on why Frémont made his next move, taking his group over the Sierra Nevada. In his memoirs, Frémont states that his decision to cross the mountains rather than the desert to the east was made because the animals were already in desperate shape. He said: "My decision was heard with great joy by the people [his men], and diffused new life throughout the camp."[116]

Traveling in deep snow, though, Frémont lost many men and animals due to the extreme weather. Of 105 horses and mules, only 33 survived. Indians along the way helped them, even providing guides, but told the explorers they would never make it through. However, by March 1844 Frémont and the remaining men arrived at Sutter's Fort in northern California.

The men had traveled thirty-five hundred miles. They had mapped the area so precisely that locations could be placed within a few feet of their actual position. When the group finally returned to Kansas Landing on July 31, 1844, Frémont's achievement was celebrated. According to historians, "His grand reconnaissance produced the first scientifically accurate map of the American West . . . and is of cardinal importance in the history of American exploration."[117]

War with Mexico

In 1845, Frémont was commissioned to make another expedition to the West. Although his orders stated that he would map several river and mountain regions, Frémont knew that at any moment it might become a military expedition as the United States was on the verge of war with Mexico over Texas and other western territories.

In the spring of 1845, Frémont entered California, stopping in Monterey to assure Mexican commandant José Castro that his expedition was strictly a scientific mapmaking mission. Castro agreed at first, but then quarreled with Frémont and ordered him to leave. During his retreat, Frémont received secret orders from the U.S. War Department in Washington, D.C. The government was declaring war on Mexico, and Frémont was to lead a military assault in California.

The Mexicans did all they could to resist the invasion. They even enlisted the Indians' help to battle Frémont's army. In response, the few American settlers in California rallied to the U.S. side by raising an army of their own. On June 14, 1846, about fifty men from these independent forces stirred up one of the most outstanding events in California history. After asking Frémont for advice, the Americans settlers raided Sonoma, California, capturing the town and raising a flag over it on which had been drawn a crude figure of a grizzly bear; they also claimed independence

Frémont knew that his mapping expedition in 1845 could become a military one at any time.

for the Republic of California. Historians still argue over whether Frémont supported or suggested this attack, but in the end, it did not matter. A few days later, Frémont arrived to take charge of the revolt. Writer Billington states, "The settlers naturally turned to Frémont . . . for protection. Regardless of whether Frémont instigated the revolt . . . his presence gave the settlers the fortitude necessary for action."[118]

Victory and a Court-Martial

Taking his army south, Frémont attacked Monterey and with the backing of the American naval forces under Commodore Robert Stockton, went on to capture that city and others, including San Francisco. Commodore Stockton then gave Frémont command of the military's ground forces.

When Brigadier General Stephen Kearny, an officer of higher rank, arrived from Arizona after losing a battle to the Mexican army, he assumed command of all forces. When Frémont balked at relinquishing control of his army, tempers flared between the two men. The situation neared the breaking point when Frémont, under orders to reoccupy Los Angeles, managed to sign a

Frémont (holding flag) takes charge of the revolt in Sonoma, California. Historians still debate whether he supported or suggested the attack.

treaty with the commander of the native Californios (Mexicans who supported independence) occupying the city. Kearny felt Frémont had overstepped his bounds—only the commanding officer had authority to sign a treaty. Furthermore, as Stockton left with his naval forces, he appointed Frémont provisional governor of California. Kearny was incensed. After all, the junior officer had become the general's superior. This became more than Kearny could bear. He arrested Frémont and took him east to be court-martialed. According to historian John Hicks, "a court-martial found [Frémont] guilty of insubordination and ordered him dismissed from the army."[119]

Even though President James Polk remitted Frémont's sentence, ordering that he be released from arrest, that his sword be returned, and that he resume active duty, Frémont refused. He resigned from the army, saying, "I feel the sentence of the court-martial against me to be unjust and while the feeling remains I can never, by any act or word whatever, even by the remotest implication, admit, or seem to admit to its justice."[120] Soon he returned to California, not to fight, but to live.

A Life in California

In mid-1848, Frémont purchased a large tract of land in California and hoped to settle down. The following year, John Charles and Jessie Frémont moved to the town of Mariposa near the Yosemite Valley. Despite his hard times, Frémont's fighting spirit and strong character remained a part of him. A writer who met him in 1849 said, "I have seen in no other man the . . . lightness, activity, strength, and physical endurance in so perfect an equilibrium. His face is rather thin and embrowned by exposure; his nose a bold aquiline [curved like an eagle's beak] and his eyes deep-set and keen as a hawk's. The rough camp-life of many years has lessened in no degree his native refinement of character and polish of manners."[121]

Soon after their arrival, the Frémonts heard that gold had been discovered at Sutter's Fort in northern California. Excited at the prospect that gold might also lie beneath his feet, Frémont began mining and discovered a rich supply. He became wealthy from the gold he found, and immediately invested it in other ventures, many of which failed.

Then in December 1849, Frémont was elected senator from California. He moved to Washington, D.C., and took his Senate seat on September 11, 1850. As a senator, Frémont began to fight for the abolition of slavery. There was a great controversy in America at the time

Despite his hard life in the wilderness, Frémont could be polished and refined, two qualities that enabled him to be elected to the Senate in 1849.

as to whether or not states should be allowed to hold slaves. Frémont believed they should not, and this made him very unpopular with large landholders who used slaves to work their land. Thus, when he returned home in 1852 to run again for senator, he lost his bid for office. Disappointed, Frémont decided to make one last expedition.

Final Expedition

Across the United States there was a cry for a railroad to connect the East and West Coasts. Frémont and Thomas Benton favored a route linking St. Louis with California along the thirty-eighth parallel and crossing the country far north of what many congressmen favored. Determined to prove his path superior, Frémont raised money and gathered a team to explore his route. By September 1853, he had recruited twenty-four men and prepared to depart from Missouri. Illness delayed them several weeks, though, and destroyed any hope of completing the trip before winter.

By November 18, 1853, the group had reached only as far west as Bent's Fort on the Arkansas River in Colorado. According to one writer, "Deep snows clogged the . . . mountain valleys of southern Colorado. . . . The . . . group slogged ahead [most] on foot. Frémont's party dissolved into a broken line of cold, half starved stragglers . . . [who] stumbled along through sleet, mud, rattlesnakes, dysentery, and scurvy."[122] The men arrived in terrible condition in San Francisco on April 16, 1854.

Even though Frémont knew the expedition had been a disaster and officials chose another route for the railroad, he published glowing reports in the newspapers trying to cover up the failure. Those were successful as his misfortune did not overshadow his former success. Author Rolle writes, "Although Frémont's last expedition was a pale facsimile [copy] of his earlier exploits, his mapmaking . . . represented an important rung on the ladder of exploration. . . . Others had preceded Frémont . . . but none became America's most charismatic pathfinder."[123]

Frémont for President

One thing did change following that failed expedition; Frémont realized his days on the trail were over. Instead, he turned his attention back to politics. In 1856, Democratic Party officials asked Frémont to run as their presidential candidate and they expected him to endorse slavery. This he could not do. A new party—the Republican Party—opposed to slavery was forming, and that same year, the Republicans asked Frémont to serve as their candidate. At the first meeting of the new party, Frémont was nominated.

Opposition to Frémont was hot. Opponents, including U.S. secretary of war Jefferson Davis, were vehemently antagonistic toward Frémont—mainly because of his opposition to slavery. Anything negative about Frémont, particularly his illegitimate birth, was published widely. Many argued that he planned to support only the northern states. Some even claimed he was a foreigner, having been born abroad. Although most of the accusations were false, many Americans believed them. Frémont lost the election, and Democrat James Buchanan became president.

An 1856 Republican Party campaign banner pictures Frémont and his running mate, William Dayton.

Still, Frémont maintained many supporters during and after the election. These people remembered his deeds of discovery many years before. A well-known scientist who knew him said of Frémont, "Columbus marked a pathway to the new-found world. Washington guided and sustained the patriots who consecrated that world . . . and Frémont lifted the

Frémont's fantastic explorations, detailed reports, and accurate maps helped settle the frontier and made him a legend.

veil which since time first began, had hidden from view [the West] the real El Dorado [mythical city of gold]."[124] Frémont's supporters asked him to run again for the presidency in 1860 and later in 1864, but Frémont was no longer interested.

In 1878, Frémont accepted a job as governor of Arizona, he did not remain there long. His frequent trips to Washington on personal business soon lost him the position. He resigned on October 11, 1881. Once again, the Frémonts moved east.

Last Years

In Washington, Frémont took on several posts. He worked as an agent for the Indians, holding power of attorney for the Cherokee regarding their rights in Texas. He wrote books about his travels and finally found a publisher for his memoirs—but that book, published in 1887, did not sell. Many researchers today believe this may have been because Frémont had been told to leave out all personal information, to write as if the story concerned another man and to end it with the court-martial. One writer says the book failed because "the memoirs concluded with 1847 . . . [and did not] account for the Pathfinder's later adventures."[125]

On July 13, 1890, the man many people called the Columbus of the West, died. Of Frémont's long and extraordinary career, one author wrote,

> Frémont's years of exploration were indeed remarkable. He covered more ground than any other government explorer, including Meriwether Lewis and William Clark. Clad in buck-

skin . . . Frémont and his men confronted dangerous natives and an untamed wilderness. . . . His scientific reports helped to dispel the myth that the western plains were the 'Great American Desert,' Frémont correctly forecast that water hidden underground, could transform the aridity of the continent's vast intermountain region. . . . Frémont's career flourished in an America that loved adventure and excitement. His spectacular exploits encouraged a legendary image.[126]

NOTES

Introduction: Inspired by American "Legends"

1. Carroll C. Calkins, ed., *The Story of America.* Pleasantville, NY: Reader's Digest, 1975, p. 68.

2. James K. Fitzpatrick, *Builders of the American Dream.* New Rochelle, NY: Arlington House, 1977, p. 11.

Chapter 1: Land, the "Magical Commodity"

3. Quoted in Bruce Lancaster, *The American Revolution.* Boston: Houghton Mifflin, 1987, p. 23.

4. Lancaster, *The American Revolution,* p. 41.

5. Thomas H. O'Connor, *The Heritage of the American People.* Boston: Allyn and Bacon, 1965, p. 75.

6. David Sievert Lavender, *The American Heritage History of the Great West.* New York: American Heritage Publishing/Bonanza Books, 1982, p. 62.

7. Quoted in Ingvard Henry Eide, ed., *An American Odyssey, the Journey of Lewis and Clark.* New York: Rand McNally, 1969, p. 2.

8. Quoted in Eide, *An American Odyssey,* p. 5.

9. Quoted in Clifford Merrill Drury, ed., *Where Wagons Could Go.* Lincoln: University of Nebraska Press, 1963, p. 53.

10. Quoted in Dee Brown, *The Westerners.* New York: Holt, Rinehart, and Winston, 1974, p. 120.

11. Calkins, *The Story of America,* pp. 81–82.

Chapter 2: Daniel Boone: Legendary American Pioneer

12. Quoted in Fitzpatrick, *Builders of the American Dream,* pp. 23–24.

13. Fitzpatrick, *Builders of the American Dream,* p. 23.

14. John Mack Faragher, *Daniel Boone, the Life and Legend of an American Pioneer.* New York: Henry Holt, 1992, p. 16.

15. Donald Culross Peattie, *Great Lives, Great Deeds.* Pleasantville, NY: Reader's Digest, 1964, p. 124.

16. Faragher, *Daniel Boone,* p. 62.

17. Quoted in Faragher, *Daniel Boone*, p. 78.

18. Faragher, *Daniel Boone*, p. 81.

19. Daniel J. Boorstin, ed., *American Civilization*. New York: McGraw-Hill, 1972, p. 30.

20. Ray Allen Billington, *Westward Expansion*. New York: Macmillan, 1965, p. 166.

21. Lavender, *The American Heritage History of the Great West*, pp. 21–22.

22. Calkins, *The Story of America*, p. 161.

23. Quoted in Faragher, *Daniel Boone*, p. 109.

24. Quoted in Calkins, *The Story of America*, p. 161.

25. Fitzpatrick, *Builders of the American Dream*, p. 40.

26. Lavender, *The American Heritage History of the Great West*, p. 36.

27. Peattie, *Great Lives, Great Deeds*, p. 129.

Chapter 3: Stephen Fuller Austin: Father of Texas

28. Billington, *Westward Expansion*, p. 485.

29. Gregg Cantrell, *Stephen F. Austin, Empresario of Texas*. New Haven, CT: Yale University Press, 1999, p. 17.

30. Cantrell, *Stephen F. Austin*, pp. 45–46.

31. Cantrell, *Stephen F. Austin*, p. 12.

32. T. R. Fehrenbach, *Lone Star, a History of Texas and the Texans*. New York: Macmillan, 1968, p. 134.

33. Quoted in Cantrell, *Stephen F. Austin*, p. 73.

34. Fehrenbach, *Lone Star*, p. 134.

35. Charles Ramsdell, *The American Heritage Book of Great Adventures of the Old West*. New York: American Heritage Press, 1969, p. 109.

36. Quoted in Cantrell, *Stephen F. Austin*, p. 90.

37. Ralph Cushman, *Jesse Chisholm*. Austin, TX: Eakins Press, 1992, p. 30.

38. Quoted in Fehrenbach, *Lone Star*, p. 138.

39. Quoted in Fehrenbach, *Lone Star*, p. 142.

40. Billington, *Western Expansion*, p. 486.

41. Quoted in Fehrenbach, *Lone Star*, p. 132.

42. Fehrenbach, *Lone Star,* p. 145.

43. Cantrell, *Stephen F. Austin,* pp. 7–8.

44. O'Connor, *The Heritage of the American People,* p. 290.

45. O'Connor, *The Heritage of the American People,* p. 290.

46. Fehrenbach, *Lone Star,* pp. 182–83.

47. Quoted in Cantrell, *Stephen F. Austin,* p. 279.

48. Quoted in Cantrell, *Stephen F. Austin,* p. 295.

49. Quoted in Fehrenbach, *Lone Star,* p. 189.

50. Quoted in Cantrell, *Stephen F. Austin,* p. 339.

51. Quoted in Cantrell, *Stephen F. Austin,* p. 356.

52. Quoted in Cantrell, *Stephen F. Austin,* p. 364.

53. Quoted in Marquis James, *The Raven, a Biography of Sam Houston.* Atlanta: Mockingbird Books, 1977, p. 227.

Chapter 4: Jedediah Smith: A Knight Wearing Buckskins

54. Billington, *Western Expansion,* pp. 557–58.

55. Dale L. Morgan, *Jedediah Smith and the Opening of the West.* Lincoln: University of Nebraska Press, 1953, p. 46.

56. Brown, *The Westerners,* p. 58.

57. Morgan, *Jedediah Smith,* pp. 91–92.

58. Quoted in Morgan, *Jedediah Smith,* p. 54.

59. Quoted in Morgan, *Jedediah Smith,* p. 54.

60. Morgan, *Jedediah Smith,* p. 82.

61. Morgan, *Jedediah Smith,* pp. 84–85.

62. Billington, *Western Expansion,* p. 458.

63. Brown, *The Westerners,* pp. 60–61.

64. Calkins, *The Story of America,* p. 167.

65. Lavender, *The American Heritage History of the Great West,* p. 127.

66. Bernard DeVoto, *Across the Wide Missouri.* Boston: Houghton Mifflin, 1947, p. 116.

67. Brown, *The Westerners,* p. 65.

68. Quoted in Morgan, *Jedediah Smith,* p. 340.

69. Quoted in Brown, *The Westerners,* p. 66.

70. Quoted in Brown, *The Westerners,* p. 68.

71. Morgan, *Jedediah Smith,* p. 7.

Chapter 5: John Augustus Sutter: Gold! In California

72. Oscar Lewis, *Sutter's Fort: Gateway to the Gold Fields.* Englewood Cliffs, NJ: Prentice-Hall, 1966, p. 7.

73. DeVoto, *Across the Wide Missouri*, pp. 350–51.

74. Lavender, *The American Heritage of the Great West*, p. 180.

75. Lewis, *Sutter's Fort*, p. 13.

76. Lewis, *Sutter's Fort*, p. 15.

77. Lavender, *The American Heritage of the Great West*, p. 217.

78. Quoted in Lewis, *Sutter's Fort*, p. 81.

79. Lewis, *Sutter's Fort*, p. 99.

80. Lewis, *Sutter's Fort*, p. 122.

81. Lewis, *Sutter's Fort*, p. 124.

82. Quoted in Lewis, *Sutter's Fort*, p. 129.

83. Quoted in Lewis, *Sutter's Fort*, p. 143.

84. Lewis, *Sutter's Fort*, p. 145.

85. John D. Hicks, *The Federal Union.* Boston: Houghton Mifflin, 1952, p. 490.

86. Lewis, *Sutter's Fort*, p. 151.

87. DeVoto, *Across the Wide Missouri*, p. 351.

Chapter 6: Narcissa Prentiss Whitman: Woman over the Mountains

88. Huston Horn, *The Pioneers.* Alexandria, VA: Time-Life Books, 1974, p. 49.

89. Horn, *The Pioneers*, p. 52.

90. Quoted in Drury, *Where Wagons Could Go*, p. 29.

91. Quoted in Drury, *Where Wagons Could Go*, p. 34.

92. Gerald F. Kreyche, *Visions of the American West.* Lexington: University Press of Kentucky, 1989, p. 190.

93. DeVoto, *Across the Wide Missouri*, p. 249.

94. Drury, *Where Wagons Could Go*, p. 50.

95. Quoted in Drury, *Where Wagons Could Go,* p. 51.

96. De Voto, *Across the Wide Missouri*, p. 247.

97. Quoted in Lawrence Dodd, *Narcissa Whitman on the Oregon Trail.* Fairfield, WA: Ye Galleon Press, 1986, p. 13.

98. Quoted in Dodd, *Narcissa Whitman on the Oregon Trail*, p. 13.

99. DeVoto, *Across the Wide Missouri,* p. 267.

100. Quoted in Dodd, *Narcissa Whitman on the Oregon Trail,* p. 11.

101. Quoted in Drury, *Where Wagons Could Go,* pp. 121–22.

102. Quoted in Drury, *Where Wagons Could Go,* p. 108.

103. Kreyche, *Visions of the American West,* p. 157.

104. DeVoto, *Across the Wide Missouri,* p. 268.

105. Quoted in Dodd, *Narcissa Whitman on the Oregon Trail,* p. 19.

Chapter 7: John Charles Frémont: Columbus of the West

106. Lavender, *The American Heritage History of the Great West,* p. 188.

107. Andrew Rolle, *John Charles Frémont, Character as Destiny.* Norman: University of Oklahoma Press, 1991, preface.

108. Quoted in Rolle, *John Charles Frémont,* p. 7.

109. Rolle, *John Charles Frémont,* p. 8.

110. Kreyche, *Visions of the American West,* p. 173.

111. Rolle, *John Charles Frémont,* p. 18.

112. Calkins, *The Story of America,* p. 76.

113. Rolle, *John Charles Frémont,* p. 39.

114. Quoted in Rolle, *John Charles Frémont,* p. 41.

115. Quoted in Rolle, *John Charles Frémont,* p. 55.

116. Quoted in Rolle, *John Charles Frémont,* p. 59.

117. Quoted in Rolle, *John Charles Frémont,* p. 65.

118. Billington, *Westward Expansion,* p. 572.

119. Hicks, *The Federal Union,* p. 481.

120. Quoted in Rolle, *John Charles Frémont,* p. 104.

121. Quoted in Rolle, *John Charles Frémont,* p. 127.

122. Rolle, *John Charles Frémont,* p. 156.

123. Rolle, *John Charles Frémont,* p. 160.

124. Quoted in Rolle, *John Charles Frémont,* p. 143.

125. Rolle, *John Charles Frémont,* p. 261.

126. Rolle, *John Charles Frémont,* preface.

FOR FURTHER READING

Wyatt Blassingame and Richard Glendinning, *Men Who Opened the West*. New York: G. P. Putnam's Sons, 1966. This book is an overview of some of the most important men who went west beginning with Francisco Vásquez de Coronado. It discusses the growth of the country from the first explorers to the Texas ranchers, and finally the railroad which helped draw the nation together.

Neta Lohnes Frazier, *Five Roads to the Pacific*. New York: David McKay, 1964. The story of the five most important expeditions that led to the opening of roads to the western United States.

Fiona MacDonald, *First Facts About the American Frontier*. New York: Peter Bedrick Books, 1996. MacDonald answers some very interesting questions about the frontier and pioneer life.

Fredrika Shumway Smith, *Frémont: Soldier, Explorer, Statesman*. New York: Rand McNally, 1966. A thorough study of John Charles Frémont and his life as an explorer and politician.

Michael V. Uschan, *Westward Expansion*. San Diego: Lucent Books, 2001. A discussion of an important period in U.S. history and the events and people which made it happen.

———, *Westward on the Oregon Trail*. New York: American Heritage Press, 1962. This is the story of people moving west and includes the adventures of Jedediah Smith, John Charles Frémont, and the Whitmans.

WORKS CONSULTED

Ray Allen Billington, *Westward Expansion*. New York: Macmillan, 1965. A detailed and interesting history of Americans as they moved westward.

Daniel J. Boorstin, ed., *American Civilization*. New York: McGraw-Hill, 1972. An overview of the building of America including maps and illustrations.

Dee Brown, *The Westerners*. New York: Holt, Rinehart, and Winston, 1974. By examining the people of the period, Brown shows not only what happened but why.

Carroll C. Calkins, ed., *The Story of America*. Pleasantville, NY: Reader's Digest, 1975. A colorful and fascinating look at America's past with pictures and sidebars full of informative material.

Gregg Cantrell, *Stephen F. Austin, Empresario of Texas*. New Haven, CT: Yale University Press, 1999. A recent biography of Stephen Austin.

Ralph Cushman, *Jesse Chisholm*. Austin, TX: Eakins Press, 1992. Chisholm was one-quarter Indian and served as a guide to many going west. He was also Sam Houston's aide during the days of Texas independence.

Bernard DeVoto, *Across the Wide Missouri*. Boston: Houghton Mifflin, 1947. A discussion of the importance of the fur trade in the West. There are also paintings of the early West by various artists.

Lawrence Dodd, *Narcissa Whitman on the Oregon Trail*. Fairfield, WA: Ye Galleon Press, 1986. A short history of Narcissa Whitman and her journey to the West.

Clifford Merrill Drury, ed., *Where Wagons Could Go*. Lincoln: University of Nebraska Press, 1963. The trip westward as seen through the personal journals of Narcissa Whitman and Eliza Spalding.

Charles T. Duncan, ed., *Horace Greeley, an Overland Journey*. New York: Alfred A. Knopf, 1964. Greeley's real-life adventure to California in 1859.

Ingvard Henry Eide, ed., *American Odyssey, the Journey of Lewis and Clark*. New York: Rand McNally, 1969. Specifically chosen portions of Lewis and Clark's diaries and letters. Filled with photography of the trail they took.

John Mack Faragher, *Daniel Boone, the Life and Legend of an American Pioneer*. New York: Henry Holt, 1992. A reliable history of the first frontiersman which separates fact from legend.

T. R. Fehrenbach, *Lone Star, a History of Texas and the Texans.* New York: Macmillan, 1968. Fehrenbach looks at Texas and its people from its beginnings to statehood.

James K. Fitzpatrick, *Builders of the American Dream.* New Rochelle, NY: Arlington House, 1977. In this well written and thoughtful book, the author chronicles the lives of thirteen Americans he calls "giants." His choices for greatness include George Washington and Walt Disney.

John Gunther, *Inside U.S.A.* New York: Harper & Brothers, 1947. A state-by-state discussion of the history of America.

Richard D. Heffner, *A Documentary History of the United States.* Bloomington: Indiana University Press, 1952. The telling of American history by the men who lived it and recorded it in their documents.

John D. Hicks, *The Federal Union.* Boston: Houghton Mifflin, 1952. A precise history of the United States until the end of the Civil War.

Huston Horn, *The Pioneers.* Alexandria, VA: Time-Life Books, 1974. An illustrated narrative of those who made the journey west before anyone else.

Marquis James, *The Raven, a Biography of Sam Houston.* Atlanta: Mockingbird Books, 1977. This Pulitzer Prize–winning biography is detailed and highly complimentary of Sam Houston, the first president of Texas.

Gerald F. Kreyche, *Visions of the American West.* Lexington: University Press of Kentucky, 1989. An in-depth examination of the reasons people—from trappers to missionaries—moved west.

Bruce Lancaster, *The American Revolution.* Boston: Houghton Mifflin, 1987. A look at the causes of the Revolutionary War and the men who fought it.

David Sievert Lavender, *The American Heritage History of the Great West.* New York: American Heritage Publishing/Bonanza Books, 1982. An informative history of the entire period from 1763 until the beginning of the twentieth century. The book is complemented with 427 pictures and maps.

Oscar Lewis, *Sutter's Fort: Gateway to the Gold Fields.* Englewood Cliffs, NJ: Prentice-Hall, 1966. Lewis tells a vivid and informative history of California during the time of John Sutter and the gold rush. He also shows the importance of Sutter's Fort as a way station for emigrants determined to settle California.

Dale L. Morgan, *Jedediah Smith and the Opening of the West.* Lincoln: University of Nebraska Press, 1953. The definitive biography of the man who saw the West first.

Samuel Eliot Morison and Henry Steele Commager, *The Growth of the American Republic*. New York: Oxford University Press, 1962. The story of America from the first European discoverer, through the foundations of its government, and the expansion of the nation until the Civil War.

Thomas H. O'Connor, *The Heritage of the American People*. Boston: Allyn and Bacon, 1965. A scholarly work covering America's entire history.

Donald Culross Peattie, *Great Lives, Great Deeds*. Pleasantville, NY: Reader's Digest, 1964. This book contains short profiles of one hundred of the world's most famous people.

Leonard Pitt, *We Americans: A Topical History of the United States*. Volume 1. Colonial Times to 1877. Glenview, IL: Scott, Foresman, 1976. Pitt explains American history by dividing it into five distinct time periods.

Charles Ramsdell, *The American Heritage Book of Great Adventures of the Old West*. New York: American Heritage Press, 1969. A collection of stories about the western experience.

Andrew Rolle, *John Charles Frémont, Character as Destiny*. Norman: University of Oklahoma Press, 1991. Rolle uses a pyschological approach to examine Frémont's character, resulting in a very unique and interesting book.

INDEX

PICTURE CREDITS

Cover Photos: Hulton Getty Collection (center), © Stock Montage, Inc. (upper right and lower left), Archive Photos (lower right)

Archive Photos, 14 (right), 70, 92

© Dave Bartruff/CORBIS, 74

© Bettmann/CORBIS, 38, 67, 72, 78, 81

© N. Carter/North Wind Picture Archives, 47

Dictionary of American Portraits, Dover Publications, Inc., 61, 86

Dictionary of American Portraits, Dover Publications, Inc./Engraved by James B. Longacre from a painting by Chester Harding, 32

Dictionary of American Portraits, Dover Publications, Inc./Engraving by John C. Buttre, 84

© FPG International, 14 (left)

© Historical Picture Archive/CORBIS, 52

Hulton Getty/Archive Photos, 26, 63, 95

Library of Congress, 11, 17, 40, 45, 57, 94

© David Muench/CORBIS, 33

© National Portrait Gallery, Smithsonian Institution/Art Resource, 96

© North Wind Picture Archives, 23, 30, 36, 39, 42, 48, 50, 54, 56, 59, 65, 79, 88, 89

Prints Old & Rare, 21, 76

© Seattle Post-Intelligencer Collection; Museum of History & Industry/CORBIS, 82

© Stock Montage, Inc., 18, 24, 29, 69, 91

ABOUT THE AUTHOR

Sherri Peel Taylor lives with her husband Jerry on the edge of the Kisatchie National Forest, near the banks of Saline Bayou in scenic north Louisiana. Mrs. Taylor's previous work for Lucent Books includes *Influential First Ladies*. Her free time is spent with her five granddaughters and on volunteer activities.